Philipp S. Müller

Unearthing the Politics of Globalization

Fragen politischer Ordnung in einer globalisierten Welt

herausgegeben von
Prof. Dr. Friedrich Kratochwil
(Universität München)

Band 4

LIT

Philipp S. Müller

Unearthing the Politics
of Globalization

LIT

Bibliographic information published by Die Deutsche Bibliothek
Die Deutsche Bibliothek lists this publication in the Deutsche
Nationalbibliografie; detailed bibliographic data are available in the
Internet at http://dnb.ddb.de.

Zugl.: München, Univ., Diss., 2003

ISBN 3-8258-6955-5

© LIT VERLAG Münster   2003
   Grevener Str./Fresnostr. 2   48159 Münster
   Tel. 0251-23 50 91   Fax 0251-23 19 72
   e-Mail: lit@lit-verlag.de   http://www.lit-verlag.de

Distributed in North America by:

Transaction Publishers
New Brunswick (U.S.A.) and London (U.K.)

Transaction Publishers   Tel.: (732) 445 - 2280
Rutgers University   Fax: (732) 445 - 3138
35 Berrue Circle   for orders (U. S. only):
Piscataway, NJ 08854   toll free (888) 999 - 6778

In Memory of Gordon Baker

Preface and Acknowledgements................................. 9

Analytical Index.. 12

Communicating Foreign Policy in a Globalizing World..... 15

THE WORLD OUTSIDE AND THE PICTURES IN OUR HEADS........ 16
"WHAT IS THE ROLE OF COMMUNICATING FOREIGN POLICY IN A
GLOBALIZING WORLD?"... 17
SKETCHING THE FIRST PROBLEM: INTERNATIONAL RELATIONS
THEORY AND COMMUNICATION 25
SKETCHING THE SECOND PROBLEM: TRANSFORMATIVE CHANGE
IN A GLOBALIZING WORLD 29
POLITICAL SCIENCE 'GOES CRITICAL' IN TIMES OF
TRANSFORMATIVE CHANGE 30
REPHRASING THE QUESTION AND OUTLINING THE ARGUMENT 34

The History of U.S. Public Diplomacy: A Catwalk of Ideas, a

Sea of Stories.. 40

A SEA OF STORIES: A HISTORICAL PERSPECTIVE ON THE
ABSTRACT PRACTICE OF PUBLIC DIPLOMACY......................... 41
PROPAGANDA IN MASS SOCIETY 46
DEMOCRATIC FOREIGN POLICY 49
EXCHANGE PROGRAMS 52
CENTRALIZATION VS. DECENTRALIZATION 54
ANTICOMMUNISM 58
COMMUNITY BASED PROGRAMS 59
INSTITUTIONALIZATION: THE UNITED STATES INFORMATION
AGENCY 60
TRUTH VS. PROPAGANDA 63

REALPOLITIK AND OTHER CRITICS 64
POST COLD WAR POLITICS: INTEGRATING USIA INTO STATE .71
CONCLUSION 73

The Political Significance of Base Metaphors in International Relations............................... 74

CRISIS: REVISITING THE FIRST PROBLEM FROM CHAPTER 1 75
WHAT DO METAPHORS DO? PUSHING BACK THE ENVELOPE ON
INTUITION 80
WHAT IS THE ROLE OF BASE METAPHORS FOR A DISCIPLINE? .85
WHAT DIFFERENTIATES THE NATURAL FROM THE SOCIAL?.....88
WHAT IS THE MAINSTREAM BASE METAPHOR IN
INTERNATIONAL RELATIONS AND WHAT DOES IT DO TO THE
DISCIPLINE? 94
WHAT ALTERNATIVES ARE THERE AND WHAT FOLLOWS FROM
THEM? 102
THE POLITICS OF BASE METAPHORS...................108
CONCLUSION 111

Imag[in]ing Globalization: Therapy for Policy Makers 113

GLOBALIZATION AND TRANSFORMATIVE CHANGE: REVISITING
THE SECOND PROBLEM OF CHAPTER 1 114
THE PROCEDURE OF PHILOSOPHICAL THERAPY...........116
SURFING THE WAVE: GLOBALIZATION AS A CAUSAL FORCE .126
DUCK-RABBIT 130
GLOCALIGRATION: GLOBAL + LOCAL, INTEGRATION +
FRAGMENTATION...................................132
SELECTION BIAS 134
CONCLUSION 136

The Politics of Communicating Foreign Policy 138

THE POLITICS OF PUBLIC DIPLOMACY 139
PUBLIC DIPLOMACY AND 9-11 145
METAPHORS AT WORK: IN SEARCH OF THE PUBLIC DIPLOMACY
PARADIGM...150
THE STATE OF THE POLICY LEVEL DEBATE 168

Conclusion: Unearthing the Politics of Globalization 172

WHAT I DID 173
VOCABULARY..175
A PLEA FOR A CRITICAL PERSPECTIVE...................................178

Bibliography 180

Preface and Acknowledgements

During times of transformative change, politics takes place on the level where we imagine the world. This level is not normally the focus of political science. My dissertation offers a framework, vocabulary, and procedure to access this level.

A dissertation is a very personal endeavor with roots that reach far back and debts not to be repaid. It is a journey that leads to unexpected but wonderful places. I foremost want to thank Friedrich Kratochwil for challenging me far beyond what I expected when I bought into this "educational journey." The doctoral program Forschungsverbund Politik-Recht-Philosophie (PRP) at the Ludwig-Maximilians-Universität München was an amazing experience. Its multidisciplinary focus and the courses by Doris Fuchs, Friedrich Kratochwil, Andreas Paulus, Julian Roberts, Bruno Simma, and Markus Zöckler have greatly influenced me and this dissertation. Our community of doctoral students with their diverse interests and common focus on communicative exchange was unique. Günther Auth, Corneliu Berari, Jörg Friedrichs, Alexandra Füller, Oliver Kessler, Markus Lederer, and Andreas Paulus were the best sparring partners for ideas imaginable. Special thanks go to the VW-foundation that found my project interesting enough to fund it. Alfred Schmidt of the VW-foundation has been a great supporter and advisor for this and our follow-up project, "Critical Perspectives on Global Governance." The German Institute for Security and International Affairs has allowed me to finish this dissertation under its wings.

I presented versions of chapter 3 of the dissertation at the Economics and Philosophy Group at Harvard University, chapter 4 at the PRP-conference in Bad Reichenhall and the "Correlates of War" seminar in Ann Arbor, and chapter 5 at ISA in New Orleans. I thank all participants for their great feedback. Special thanks go to David Ronfeldt who invited me to his wonderful house in Manhattan Beach to talk through some of the ideas.

I was lucky enough to be taught by very special professors in Georgetown, Munich, and Venice. I want to thank Chris Achen, Tony Arend, Gordon Baker, Andy Bennett, David Kennedy, and Ned Lebow for their efforts. The progress I made in the last years would not have been possible without them, my fellow-students such as Becky Johnson, Jason Davidson, Thomas Teichler, my students from Georgetown, Munich, and the Wayne State Junior Year Abroad Program that served as guinea pigs for my fledgling ideas, Mareile, my family, and friends like Bea, Christian, Ortholf, and Thomas.

My research assistants, Simon Stein and Katie Tobin, did much more than help me with the editing. Together we went through the argument countless times and if it has become clear it is because of them. With Katie based in Oregon, the sun (almost) never set on our efforts.

I want to dedicate this dissertation to the memory of Gordon Baker, who introduced me to the concept of philosophical therapy and will always be remembered by those of us who were fortunate enough to know him and learn from him.

Philipp S. Müller
Berlin, 16 May 2003

Analytical Index

The aim of this dissertation is to introduce a way of thinking that allows us to understand globalization by (re)politicizing it. A number of very abstract questions will need to be addressed because in times of transformative change, politics takes place on the level where we imagine the world. Accessing this level by engaging the policy maker is the responsibility of the political scientist.

Chapter I
In the first chapter I pose the question, "What is the role of communicating foreign policy in a globalizing world?," outline some of the problems with this question, sketch strategies to deal with them, and reformulate the question into: "How can we, on a conceptual level, describe and access the politics that are taking place in this time of transformative change in the abstract practice of communicating foreign policy?"

Chapter II
Chapter two outlines the development of communicating foreign policy in the 20th century, showing how historical arguments influence the abstract practice of public diplomacy. Focusing on the history of public diplomacy enables us to reflect on how we currently use the concept and on how this usage has developed, thus putting contemporary

arguments in perspective and permitting a critical examination of the vocabulary and concepts that policy makers use.

Chapter III

In chapter three, I analyze the conceptual foundations of international relations and how they impact our ability to ascribe meaning to foreign policy instruments such as the communication of foreign policy. The question driving this chapter is to find out how base metaphors shape the practice of international relations, especially by obscuring existing political options. I argue that a shift is taking place from the metaphor of the international system as a Hobbesian state of nature to an Aristotelian language community.

Chapter IV

In chapter four, I introduce a technique that allows us to reveal the political dimension of base metaphors by engaging the policy maker in a therapeutic relationship. I use the example of how policy makers perceive globalization, because that example also enables us to understand the political opportunities of global transformative change. The technique I propose is called *philosophical therapy*, a four step procedure based on the work of Ludwig Wittgenstein.

Chapter V

In chapter five, I focus on the policy level communicating foreign policy, applying the type of perspective developed in the preceding chapters. I analyze the U.S. public diplomacy discourse in the aftermath of the September 11, 2001, terrorist attacks, focusing on the metaphors and general concepts policy makers use to explain their investment in public diplomacy.

Chapter VI
In chapter six, I sum up my findings and conclude that the developments outlined in the preceding chapters need to be addressed by political science. A critical policy science is necessary.

Communicating Foreign Policy in a Globalizing World

In this introductory chapter I pose the question, "What is the role of communicating foreign policy in a globalizing world?," outline some of the problems with this question, sketch strategies to deal with them, and reformulate the question into: "How can we, on a conceptual level, describe and access the politics that are taking place in this time of transformative change in the abstract practice of communicating foreign policy?"

To traverse the world men must have maps of the world.
Their persistent difficulty is to secure maps on which their own
need, or someone else's need, has not sketched in the coast of Bo-
hemia.
(Lippman 1922)

The World Outside and the Pictures in our Heads

Sometimes, trying to answer a question leads to new problems worth considering. This introductory chapter starts
out with such a question: "What is the role of communicating foreign policy in a globalizing world?" It seems to be an
innocent empirical question. I will address it by (a) sketching the role of communication for U.S. foreign policy, (b)
scanning international relations theory for what it might be
able to say on the issue, and (c) sketching the enormous
transformative change that our world is currently experiencing. This approach will confront me with a number of
epistemic, theoretical and politico-philosophical problems
which I believe must be considered in the context of my
analysis, and which will lead me to question some of the
basic principles of political science. We will find that, due
to the abstract dimension of the issue, the inability of mainstream international relations to conceptualize communication, and policy makers' view of today's international
realm as in a state of flux, we cannot simply answer the
question by relying on the conventional tools of the policy
sciences.

These problems make it necessary to amend the original question so that we can introduce a number of relevant distinctions: "How can we, on a conceptual level, access and describe the political moves that are taking place in this time of transformative change in the abstract practice of communicating foreign policy?"

To tackle this question, I will propose a framework that allows us to describe the political dimension of imagining the international realm as well as a procedure to influence the political elites that make these decisions.

"What is the Role of Communicating Foreign Policy in a Globalizing World?"

Public diplomacy, the communication of U.S. foreign policy, is a field of foreign policy under which information services, education, cultural exchanges, and international broadcasting are subsumed. In essence, public diplomacy is a government activity designed to generate foreign support for U.S. policies. Coordinated by the State Department, it is also executed under other government agencies, including the Defense Department. Significant programs include academic and professional exchange programs such as Fulbright grants, government-run wire services and Internet sites such as the Washington File, and radio broadcast services including the Voice of America and Radio Free Europe/Radio Liberty. Public diplomacy is an *abstract practice*, i.e. it does not exist independently of policy makers categorizing disparate concrete programs such as student exchanges and international broadcasting as one coherent abstract policy (chapter 2). Consequently, the concept of public diplomacy varies internationally. Germany, for example, uses the term *foreign cultural policy* and does not assign direct strategic relevance to it, in contrast to policy makers in the U.S. (Dizard 2001). However, the term is becoming fashionable in global foreign ministries (Brown 2002).

According to a Library of Congress study of U.S. international and cultural programs and activities, the term *public diplomacy* originates from the 1965 establishment of the Fletcher School's Edward R. Murrow Center for Public Diplomacy (Tuch 1990, 8). A Fletcher document, quoted in <u>Communicating with the World: U.S. Public Diplomacy Overseas</u> by Hans Tuch (1990), describes public diplomacy as focusing on

> the role of the press and other media in international affairs, cultivation by governments of public opinion, the non-governmental interaction of private groups and interests in one country with those of another, and the impact of these transnational processes on the formulation of policy and the conduct of foreign affairs.

In a more forceful tone, the Reagan administration in the National Security Decision Directive 77 (Management of Public Diplomacy Relative to National Security) of January 14, 1983, defined public diplomacy as "actions of the government designed to generate support for our national security objectives".[1] This aggressive definition was counter-balanced by the State Department's 1988 definition: "Public diplomacy is 20th century public affairs, adapting traditional approaches both domestically and abroad to take account of modern communications technology."[2]

Hans Tuch, a career foreign service professional, describes the field as "A government's process of communicating with foreign publics in an attempt to bring about understanding for its nation's ideas and ideals, its institutions and culture, as well as its national goals and current policies" (Tuch 1990, 3). More recently, the Clinton administration called public diplomacy, "the action of engaging foreign audiences and opinion makers, through information and exchange programs, to advance U.S. national interests and strategic goals."[3]

The large number of different definitions shows that no generally accepted description of public diplomacy exists. Tensions appear between different frameworks conceptualizing public diplomacy, between public diplomacy as propaganda or as information, between short-term and long-term goals, and between public diplomacy as a strategic instrument of security policy or as a stand-alone issue, which means that the politics of public diplomacy takes-place on a conceptual level (chapter 3).

---

[1] NSDD-77, http://www.fas.org/irp/offdocs/nsdd/nsdd-077.htm.
[2] Department of State. "Office of Public diplomacy." State. January 1988, 53.
[3] USIA. USIA Strategic Plan 1997 – 2002. Washington, 1997.

Communicating Foreign Policy and Globalization

Following recent publications such as Mark Leonard's <u>Britain</u>™ (1997) and <u>Public Diplomacy</u> (2002), Peter van Ham's "The Rise of the Brand State" in <u>Foreign Affairs</u>, and John Arquilla and David Ronfeldt's <u>Noopolitik</u> (1999), public diplomacy has been perceived as a field that will grow in importance because of the development of information and communication technologies and the shift of political power to publics (Chapter 5). This view is shared in the United States Advisory Commission on Public Diplomacy's report, <u>Publics and Diplomats in the Global Communications Age</u>: "In this age of information and democratization, of Internet and globalized markets, publics are far more powerful than ever. Publics, through elections, demonstrations, and nongovernmental organizations, can have a profound effect on their governments' foreign policy". (US Advisory Commission on Public Diplomacy 1998) President William J. Clinton argued that, "as we move from the Industrial to the Information Age, from the Cold War world to the global village, we have an extraordinary opportunity to advance our values at home and around the world." (1998)

It is therefore necessary to ask, "What is the role of U.S. public diplomacy in a globalizing world?" At first glance, this question seems concrete, sensible, and answerable. It seems to suggest that we need to evaluate the efficacy of

20

public diplomacy and changes in the international realm that might have an influence on it in the future.

Competing Concepts

However, the situation is more complex than that. Public diplomacy's rise to fame is not uncontested. Public diplomacy, on the one hand, seems to be gaining momentum with economic globalization and the developments in information and communication technologies. The George W. Bush administration argues in its <u>National Security Strategy of the United States of America</u> that public diplomacy will play an increasing role in its foreign policy.[4] Yet on the other hand, the expenditures for public diplomacy are still far below the 1990 levels. The traditionally well-funded United States Information Agency (USIA) has had its budget cut by almost one third since 1990, U.S. public diplomacy programs such as libraries and cultural resource centers have been dismantled worldwide, and in 1998 USIA was officially merged with the State Department, supposedly to put public diplomacy at the center of foreign policy, but with little success.[5] The early Bush administra-

---

[4] http://www.whitehouse.gov/nsc/nss.html.
[5] See for example the "testimony of Joseph Duffey, Director, USIA before the Subcommittee on Commerce, Justice, State, Judiciary and Related Agencies Committee on Appropriations, House of Representatives February 26, 1998," Washington: Government Printing Office, 1998.

tion continued the trend by assigning minimal importance to the issue.

After September 11, 2001, as Arabs where cheering in the streets at the collapse of the World Trade Center, it became shockingly clear that U.S. public diplomacy had not been successful. Although the debate on the future of U.S. public diplomacy has intensified since then, the discussion is still centered more on how we should conceptualize public diplomacy than on specific policy choices (chapter 5).

This means a closer look at the competing concepts should be interesting. However, to do that we will have to deal with two major problems. First, how we conceptualize public diplomacy determines to a large extent its relevance. Mainstream international relations theory cannot "see" phenomena such as public diplomacy, which involve non-signaling communication, because this exclusion of communication delineates it from political theory and legitimizes its uniqueness (Walker 1993). Seen from this perspective, public diplomacy is useless, maybe even a waste of resources.

Second, if we accept the (globalizing) world to be in transformative change, the concepts we use to describe and explain international behavior might not fit the actual international behavior anymore (Lippman 1920). We need to critically examine our concepts of the world, and especially the policy makers' concepts, since they are responsible for shaping the international realm by acting according to certain basic assumptions about its nature, thus continually (re)creating international relations (chapter 3).

Conceptual Difficulties

These related problems lead to such questions as: Why is it difficult for international relations theory to describe and explain the communication of foreign policy? Why are policy makers confused about communicating foreign policy? What do policy makers assume when they argue for or against the relevance of communicating foreign policy? To what extent do these assumptions already determine their answers? How appropriate are these assumptions in times of transformative change? Who decides what is the "right" description of the international realm? How can we describe the politics of deciding on the right description? Who is competent to describe the international realm? How can we introduce accountability?

These questions show that it is necessary to focus primarily on our conceptual difficulties in dealing with public diplomacy. However, this changes the focus of the inquiry from looking at the effectiveness of one instrument of foreign policy to a more general conceptual musing. I believe this change of focus to be legitimate because in times of transformative change, such musings are of great political relevance (chapter 3).

This reflection must then deal with core assumptions of international relations theory and policy making. I will start out by introducing a simple but very useful distinction. I will differentiate between the *theory level* and the *policy level* in international relations, in order to distinguish between the level where international relations are observed, for example by political scientists, and the policy level where the international realm is imagined and (re)produced through acts by policy makers (chapter 3). I should point out that there is a certain interdependence between the two levels, since what happens on the policy level influences political theory, and political theory in turn participates in shaping the image that policy makers have of the world.

I will focus in this analysis on how the policy makers' imaginations influence policy making. To answer this question, I will use a linguistic concept called *metaphorology* (chapter 3) that will allow me to argue that some of the discomfort voiced by both theorists and policy makers concerning public diplomacy is the result of the changes that we are experiencing on the foundational level of our thinking. In order to open up possibilities for influencing how policy makers see the world, I will propose to the policy advisor the technique of *philosophical therapy* (chapter 4). But first, I will explain how international relations theory conceptualizes the communication of foreign policy, and secondly, how our concepts hold up in times of transformative change.

Sketching the First Problem: International Relations Theory and Communication

The mainstream base metaphor of international relations is the Hobbesian 'state of nature,' conceptualized as anarchy, or more precisely as anomy (chapter 3). International relations as a full-fledged academic discipline is based on the distinction between the inside, the hierarchically structured nation-state, and the outside, the anomic realm of relations between equal nation-states. This distinction allowed the founders of international relations to infer a different logic for international coaction and justify the need for a new academic discipline (Walker 1993). The Hobbesian state of nature image is responsible for the fact that, to this day, mainstream international relations theories have problems conceptualizing public diplomacy, because in an anomic playing field communication can only take place via action, and not via language. In Hobbes' state of nature, individuals, and, on the international level, states, are participants in a permanent prisoner's dilemma – nobody can be trusted, thus actions are the only reliable source of information about the other's intentions (chapter 3). International relations theories based on this metaphor therefore tend to oppose attaching significance to international communication via language. These problems stemming from the sociology of the scientific discipline impede the integration of public diplomacy into international relations. Public diplomacy assumes truth discourses and communicative realms to make its claims, concepts which need to be excluded in mainstream international relations in order to delineate the international from national levels. Mainstream international relations theory has so far not been interested in questions of language and communication (chapter 3).

While political theory inside the state deals with the achievement of the good life, survival in the international realm is assured by balancing capabilities (Waltz 1979). While political theory deals with non clear-cut normative issues, international relations is able to rely on a clean "natural science" approach, because actors' choice of action in the international system is so restrained by the structural constraints of the anarchic system that it can be excluded, just as economists do not have to focus on the individual choice of a seller to set a price in a perfectly competitive market (Waltz 1979, 90). This view has never been the only image shaping international relations, although it has been seminal in the mainstream discourse (Keohane 1986,). These approaches, commonly referred to as *(neo-)realism* and *(neo-)liberalism* have had an important influence on international relations theory even though they have a less than successful track record in describing, explaining, or predicting international outcomes (chapter 3). Mainstream international relations can only conceptualize public diplomacy as epiphenomenal, because by postulating an anarchic international realm, realism excludes meaningful communication via language a priori. Not allowing for language is what makes international relations special and a discipline distinct from domestic political theory (chapter 3).

Mainstream international relations has survived both theoretical and empirical challenges almost unscathed (Baldwin 1993). Realism, which has been the predominant discourse for a very long time, has marginalized important phenomena in international relations such as norms, international law, and communication by assumption, even though other perspectives have always existed (Kratochwil 1989).

However, realism has recently hit an empirical and an epistemic challenge: globalization seems to lead to foreign policies that place greater emphasis on the political persuasion of foreign publics in order to build support for the acceptance of states' international actions (Held 1995).

Paralleling this development, the relationship between norm-governed, strategic, and communicative action has become one of the most significant recent debates in the field of international relations. The introduction of communicative action into mainstream international relations theory has given us tools to analyze phenomena that up to now have been below the radar of our conceptual frameworks (Risse 2000). Public diplomacy is such a phenomenon that can only be understood if we accept deliberation or rational argumentation as one of the modes of international interaction. However, it does not yet play a major role as an empirical field to be observed by scholars.

In order to have a meaningful discourse about public diplomacy, misunderstandings, misconceptions, and inconsistencies must be dissolved and the foundation of the discipline must be revisited (chapter 3).

Sketching the Second Problem: Transformative Change in a Globalizing World

Global economic integration, the development of information and communication technologies, and the end of the Cold War have left international relations in a state of puzzlement. The relationship between our theories and "the world out there" (Lippman 1920) is in question. The field of policy making is sprouting new, conflicting with theories of how we imagine world order. During times of transformative change, much of the politics takes place on the level where we imagine the world. The European perspective imagines a world structured by global legalization (Simma, Paulus 2001), while the U.S. perspective imagines an approaching global anarchy with warrior leaders and coalitions of the willing ordering the world in ad hoc fashion (Kaplan 1994, 2001). In order to regain an understanding, we need to focus on the concepts we use, their implications, how they influence the practice of international relations, and what politics are involved (chapter 4). This critical perspective is different from the classical critical project, since it is not driven by the interest to uncover hidden power structures, but by an epistemic need to regain an understanding of what is happening around us.

Political Science 'Goes Critical' in Times of Transformative Change

International relations is a contested discipline. The reliance on anomy as the foundational feature of international relations and the practical need for concepts based on causality and determinism in order to explain and predict cannot easily be brought into conformity with the assumption that our objects of analysis are reflective decision makers who can imagine their world and decide to participate in collective institutions (Wendt 1999).

Therefore, the focus of the discipline lies as much on disciplinary-reflective questions as on substantive problems of international relations (Zalewski 1996). Conventional critical approaches reflect upon our usage of concepts in order to evaluate their usefulness and offer alternatives. Up until now, however, critical theory in international relations has mainly focused on the sociology of knowledge in the discipline in order to uncover the political motives behind epistemic positions (Neufeld 1995). The tool used was mainly the critical analysis of the self-understanding of the discipline by deconstructing the three debates (realism vs. idealism, behaviorism vs. historicism, and positivism vs. post-positivism) as the modes of construction of knowledge in the discipline (Thies 2002). In this endeavor, critical theorists have captured the political issues at stake very well (Der Derian, Shapiro 1989). And in times when the world is undergoing transformative change, this type of inquiry becomes ever more important -

- when the world changes we need to critically reflect our conceptual tools.

However, critical theorists often have missed an important aspect of this relationship. They have ignored the policy level and its relevance for the discipline of international relations. This problem stems from the inherent modesty of critical approaches. They focus on the discipline of international relations without taking into account the relationship between international relations and international policy makers. This assumption of academic irrelevance is dangerous, however. International relations on the policy level is an abstract practice, and the images in a limited number of policy makers' heads form the basis of policy making. Therefore, the critical perspective of mainstream international relations thinking needs to focus on the theory-policy frontier. By questioning accepted world views, the political relevance of a decision for one particular description of the world can be revealed to policy makers and their principals.

Before we delve any deeper into international relations theory, we should understand our actors. *Policy makers* are actors who "create" the world by persuading their principals to accept a certain description of it, and by then acting according to the consequences their description implies. *Principals* is used here as the generic term for the individuals and groups that policy makers represent, as in principal-agent theorizing (Spence and Zeckhauser, 1971; Ross 1973). The relationship between principal and policy maker can be legal, moral, or political. *Politics* can therefore be defined as decision making by policy makers, via their imag-

31

ining communities and their worlds, and by persuading principals within these imagined worlds and communities of the necessity a of certain perspectives or actions. Policy makers persuade others that something is one way or another, in the interest of their common social community, by fiat, etc. (Weber 1974) This deliberately broad definition of politics and policy makers is derived from the epistemic assumption of the freedom of our objects of analysis. Policy makers in international relations need to have three abilities: to assume their own decision making capacity, to imagine themselves as different from others yet interdependent, and to be able to see themselves as part of collectivities and intersubjective worlds.

When we want to describe, explain, and predict these actors' behaviors, we rely on vocabulary and argumentative moves that have a deterministic bias, such as causation and structural determinism. Two tricks can help us deal with this deterministic bias: questioning our basic assumptions and argumentative moves (*critical theory*), and focusing on the foundational level of analysis where policy makers imagine their world, thereby uncovering and recovering the politics of imagining the international realm (chapter 3).

Uncovering/recovering the political realm refers to the act of (a) increasing the freedom of policy makers to reach decisions by pointing out to them that they have choices in contexts where they believe to be restrained by necessity (Sachzwang), and (b) holding policy makers accountable to their principles and thereby empower their principals. My approach differs from classic critical projects: As I have already pointed out, the thrust of my inquiry does not come from the thrill of uncovering hidden power structures (Foucault 1972), but from the belief that transformative change forces us to reevaluate the concepts describing and explaining the globalizing world, as Wallerstein argues in The End of the World As We Know It: Social Science for the Twenty-First Century (1999). Only by reflecting upon the concepts of both theorists and policy makers will it be possible to uncover and recover the political aspects of globalization (chapter 3).

I will do this by taking the "easy case" (Eckstein 1975) of public diplomacy, a foreign policy field that should increase in importance with globalization, and tackle the problems that arise when we look at the issue more closely. My main point will be that the instruments of the classic policy sciences cannot handle the most interesting aspects of the issue. During times of transformative change, much of the politics takes place on the level of where we imagine the world. In order to describe politics on this level, I offer metaphorology as a framework to unearth the politics of transformative change, and philosophical therapy as a technique to access policy makers.

Rephrasing the Question and Outlining the Argument

I have taken a subfield of foreign policy, public diplomacy, as an interesting empirical study for how U.S. foreign policy is evolving during times of transformative change. However, when looking closer at the issue area, we will find that we are confronted with two problems:

International relations on the theory and policy levels have difficulties in conceptualizing public diplomacy. This can be traced to the foundational decision of international relations to define the international realm as the anomic outside to a hierarchical inside.

During times of transformative change, a gap exists between our concepts and the world, and acts of re-imagining the world must take place. These new formulations are hidden political acts. Only if their political relevance is taken into account can we improve policy makers' options and make them accountable to their principals.

Therefore, there is no simple answer to my question regarding the role of public diplomacy in a globalizing world. We must instead ask, "How can we deal with this type of question?" It very soon becomes clear that our question is to a large extent on a conceptual level, the level where policy makers (with the help of theorists) imagine their world. Such conceptual questions are not politically innocent. We need to examine how the practice of public diplomacy has developed over time, offer a framework to describe the politics on this conceptual level, and devise a technique to access policy makers. Once this is completed, it becomes necessary to assess if the inquiry has a value beyond this specific question, and if it is applicable to other questions in international relations during times of transformative change.

The two decisive analytical instruments in this inquiry are *metaphorology* and *philosophical therapy*. Metaphorology, as I use it, unearths political choices that are taken prior to any investigation or decision in international relations by analyzing basic assumptions implicit in the images and categories used to describe both the international realm and concrete policies. In essence, metaphorology offers a way to describe the politics of imagining the world.

These political choices are made in historic contexts by "real" people and therefore we can confront policy makers over these choices. The approach offered to policy advisors is philosophical therapy, a technique analogous to psychoanalytical therapy that enables us to increase the margin of choice policy makers have, and to make them accountable to their principals.

Obviously, the empirical question, "What is the role of public diplomacy in a globalizing world?" has led us to problems worth contemplating. The agenda for this analysis can now be formulated as follows: "How can we describe and access the political moves that are taking place in this time of transformative change on the conceptual level of the abstract practice of public diplomacy?"

My analysis is structured in the following way: In this introductory chapter I posed a question, outlined some of the problems with this question, and sketched strategies to deal with them.

Chapter two asks how the field of public diplomacy has developed in the 20th century in order to trace how historical arguments influence present and future public diplomacy. Focusing on the history of public diplomacy enables us to put contemporary arguments in perspective and critically examine the subject's vocabulary and concepts.

In chapter three, I analyze the conceptual foundations of international relations and how they impact our ability to ascribe meaning to foreign policy instruments such as public diplomacy. The question driving this chapter is to find out what base metaphors do and how they shape the practice of international relations, in order to uncover and recover the political questions that need to be addressed before we can begin to talk in depth about public diplomacy. I do this by arguing that the base metaphors we use to describe and explain international relations are not innocent, but rather delineate the type of research and actions we can take. I argue that a shift on this most basic level is taking place, and the metaphor of the international system as a Hobbesian state of nature is being superseded by an Aristotelian language community. This has to be done carefully, because the vocabulary to deal with this type of critical inquiry has not yet been introduced to international relations, and the base metaphor of the Hobbesian state of nature is more deeply entrenched than we often realize.

In chapter four, I introduce a technique that allows us to access the politics of base metaphors by therapeutically engaging the policy maker. I will focus on how policy makers perceive globalization, because this better enables us to understand the politics of transformative change that is taking place. Philosophical therapy enables us to deal with grammatical problems, i.e. problems of the usage of language. Globalization depoliticizes by restraining the range of decisions political actors can make. Therefore, the task for the politically-minded is clear: It is our responsibility to regain political territory and open up political spaces--to essentially uncover and recover the political realm. This can be done by pointing at contexts that in the traditional narrative are considered unproblematic or determined, but that hide political decisions. I do this by proposing the four-step technique of philosophical therapy, which (a) challenges a dogma, (b) exposes a picture that stands behind this dogma, (c) proposes an alternative picture of concept-application, and (d) deflects anxieties about this new model. By doing so, I offer a range of options to policy makers and make them accountable to their principles and principals.

In chapter five, I focus on the empirics of public diplomacy in a globalizing world. I analyze the public diplomacy discourse in the aftermath of the September 11, 2001, terrorist attacks. I will focus on the metaphors policy makers use to explain their investment in public diplomacy. There is not one main metaphor defining the policy field, however. A tension exists between conceptualizations that aim at strategic influence and conceptualizations that aim for communicative dialogue. If we use the discourse on public diplomacy to judge the U.S. foreign policy makers' understanding of the international system, we can deduce that policy makers have moved beyond a realpolitik approach, and towards a global framework. However, by talking about soft power as an extension of the realpolitik framework (Nye 2002), they do not show great appreciation for fostering a communicative realm. Yet that is exactly what would be necessary to deal with a rising number of global problems.

Globalization is challenging traditional academic analysis and conventional policy making. In chapter six, I conclude that these developments must be addressed by the policy sciences. If during times of transformative change, much of the politics takes place on the level where we imagine the world, a critical policy science is necessary, which means a new agenda for the policy advisor. The technological and cultural transformations we are experiencing as citizens, academics, and policy makers cannot be explained within the limits of our traditional modes of thinking.

In order to understand the future of public diplomacy, an issue area closely intertwined with globalization, we need to ask how we use concepts and what follows from our usage. In times of transformative change, any question about issues such as public diplomacy whose praxis and political relevance largely depend on how they are conceptualized becomes a conceptual question, and can only be answered if we focus on policy makers' imagination of the world. In order to describe politics on this level, I reflect on the future of foreign policy instruments such as public diplomacy and the capacity of states to make political decisions in the 21st century.

The History of U.S. Public Diplomacy: A Catwalk of Ideas, a Sea of Stories

This chapter outlines the development of public diplomacy in the 20th century in order to show how historical arguments influence the abstract practice public diplomacy. Focusing on the history of public diplomacy enables us to reflect on how we currently use the concept and on how this usage has developed, thus putting contemporary arguments in perspective and permitting a critical examination of the vocabulary and concepts that policy makers use.

He looked into the water and saw that it was made up of a thousand thousand thousand and one different currents, each one of a different colour, weaving in and out of one another like a liquid tapestry of breathtaking complexity; and Iff explained that these were the Streams of Story, that each coloured strand represented and contained a single tale. Different parts of the Ocean contained different sorts of stories, and as all the stories that had ever been told and many that were still in the process of being invented could be found here, the Ocean of the Streams of Story was in fact the biggest library in the universe. And because the stories were held here in fluid form, they retained the ability to change, to become new versions of themselves, to join up with other stories an so become yet other stories; so that unlike a library of books, the Ocean of the Streams of Story was much more than a storeroom of yarns.

(Rushdie 1990)

A Sea of Stories: A Historical Perspective on the Abstract Practice of Public Diplomacy

This chapter asks how the field of public diplomacy developed in the 20th century in order to trace how historical arguments influence the present and future of public diplomacy. Focusing on the history of public diplomacy enables us to put contemporary arguments in perspective and criti-

41

cally examine its vocabulary and concepts. I will proceed chronologically in order to avoid confusion about the evolution of institutions and programs that resulted from the different concepts applied.

When we use the term 'public diplomacy' we make arguments on a high level of abstraction: It is a concept used to describe disparate policies and ascribe strategic value to their combined effects. This means that if we want to understand the present state and predict the future of public diplomacy we have to reflect on how we use the concept and how this usage has developed (Bartelsen 1995).

Although public diplomacy has played an important role in foreign policy, it only recently has caught the interest of the academic discipline of international relations (Ninkovich 1996; Leonard 1999, 2002; Dizard 2001; Potter 2002). I will argue in the next chapter that this can be explained by the fact that the base metaphor of the discipline, the Hobbesian state of nature, excludes questions about communicative realms. In contrast to government-to-government diplomacy, development policy, nuclear strategy, or international organizations, public diplomacy has not developed an academic discourse paralleling the policy discourse. Therefore, I will focus on the history of the public diplomacy policy discourse using mainly primary and non-academic sources.

It is important to distinguish between an abstract policy discourse and an academic discourse because they function differently. Even though they might be on similar levels of abstraction, different claims will be allowed as legitimate arguments and over time the discourses develop according to different patterns. The criteria of validity for making claims in the discourses are different, at least in theory: An academic discourse posits a complete description of a phenomena, the development of a system of hypotheses, the derivation of further hypotheses, the description of a language of observation for the community, the observation of the phenomena found by the position of hypotheses, and the accumulation of results derived by this process. This process of knowledge accumulation is then described either locally as *normal science* (Kuhn 1950), *debates* (Lapid 1989), or what could be referred to as *pseudo-debates* in Cameron G. Thies. "Progress, History and Identity in International Relations Theory: The Case of the Idealist- Realist Debate" (Thies 2002).

Policy makers use a more associational style of argument. Concepts that have a certain ad hoc plausibility to policy makers or their constituents are utilized to make legitimating claims for positions or actions. A surprising new argument can persuade, and old arguments are forgotten and sometimes later reintroduced. Consistency in an argument has a different role in ascribing validity than in the academic discourse. The cumulative building of knowledge is not at the core of policy imagery. Different ways of describing such a discourse are necessary. Recounting the historical narrative of the abstract political debates on public diplomacy therefore cannot be done by referring to discrete debates that build on each other.

I view the conceptual development of public diplomacy as being rather similar to the fashion industry, where at different points in time, different designs are considered in

43

or out of fashion-- where we do not expect progressive development, but surprising nuances and sometimes radical inventions.

Concepts that we will come upon again and again in the discourse on public diplomacy, as we keep seeing variations of pants and skirts in the realm of fashion, include propaganda and mass society theories, the democratic peace argument, behaviorism, American exceptionalism, realist international relations theories, and branding. Even though these concepts are on different epistemic levels, they are used to make claims in the political discourse with similar legitimating force. In the next paragraphs I will outline them in their ideal-typical forms in which they are not found in the wild.

Propaganda theory and the theory and experience of mass society have greatly influenced the public diplomacy debates of the 20th century. Harold Lasswell argues, "Propaganda is the control of opinion by significant symbols, or, so to speak, more concretely and less accurately by stories, rumors, reports, pictures, and other forms of social communication." (Lasswell 1922) He qualifies the relevance of the term propaganda by arguing, "There is a need for a word which means the making of a deliberately one-sided statement to a mass audience. Let us choose 'propaganda' as such a word" (Lasswell 1922).

The Kantian *democratic peace argument* has come up in different manifestations, as cosmopolitanism before World War I, as Wilsonian idealism, as aggressive democratic expansionism in the Reagan administration, or as transformation cottage industry in the Clinton administration. This

44

dispute about public diplomacy, understood as propaganda on the one hand and democratic diplomacy with the goal of achieving world peace on the other, lies at the heart of many debates on public diplomacy.

Behaviorism has had a great influence on public diplomacy, both in supporting the argument that stimulus-response models can describe the practice of public diplomacy, and as a methodological ideology that has strongly influenced the evaluation methods of the 2003 budget of the Bush administration.[6]

Of course, any U.S. foreign policy is influenced by the script of *American exceptionalism*, founded on the John Winthrop's 'City upon a Hill' sermon, interpreted either in its isolationist or interventionist streak.

Realpolitik, or realist thinking, is deeply entrenched in U.S. foreign policy making. It is based on the Hobbesian state of nature metaphor and argues that public diplomacy is epiphenomenal. Its strength might be explained by the usurpation of the term *realism*, organizational inertia in the universities, or the simplistic elegance of the concept.

Branding is based on the idea of linking products to communities that are created by commercial organizations. This concept has permeated social life to the point that thinking in terms of "unbranded" products or services is nearly impossible (Klein 1999).

---

[6] The Bush administration Budget document "Governing with Accountability" can be found at:
http://www.whitehouse.gov/omb/budget/fy2003/budget.html. The specific data for the State Department can be found at:
http://www.whitehouse.gov/omb/budget/fy2003/bud20.html.

Observing the changes in public diplomacy through time can give us a perspective on it and can give us a first understanding of how we use the concept. In the following section, I will focus on the field as it has developed through time, using history as a metaphorical catwalk for the very abstract concepts that play a relevant role in the contemporary debate on and practice of public diplomacy.

Propaganda in Mass Society

Early public diplomacy can be understood simply as propaganda. According to Harold Lasswell (1922), "Propaganda is the control of opinion by significant symbols ... by stories, rumors, reports, pictures, and other forms of social communication." The term *propaganda* is first mentioned in the Sacred Congregation de Propaganda Fide, which is the department of the pontifical administration charged with the spread of Catholicism and with the regulation of ecclesiastical affairs in non-Catholic countries (Condignola 1991).

This academic focus on propaganda was induced by the realization that the U.S. is a mass society requiring a system of mass communication (Beniger 1987). In turn, this realization of a society that imagines itself not through direct physical interaction, as had been the imagery up to the early twentieth century, but through media and symbols, led to the study of these types of phenomena by such authors as Lasswell and Lippman (1922).

46

President Woodrow Wilson established the Committee on Public Information, Propaganda, and Psychological Warfare (CPI) on April 13, 1917, shortly after the United States entered World War I (Mock, Larson 1939). The Journalist George Creel was named chairman of the committee, which was referred to as the Creel Committee.

George Creel argued in On Selling the War (1920), "There was no part of the great war machinery that we did not touch, no medium of appeal that we did not employ. The printed word, the spoken word, the motion picture, the telegraph, the cable, the wireless, the poster, the sign-board - all these were used in our campaign to make our own people and all other peoples understand the causes that compelled America to take arms." Until the end of the war, it was the CPI's task to inform American citizens, and the world in general, about the democratic goals of U.S. policy and about the threat to the world posed by the imperialistic goals of the enemy states. The committee mobilized an immense communication network of newspapers, radio, motion pictures, rail lines, telegraph cables, automobiles, and public speakers. Creel describes one of these measures as the Four Minute Men: "The Four Minute Men, an organization that will live in history by reason of its originality and effectiveness, commanded the volunteer services of 75,000 speakers, operating in 5,200 communities, and making a total of 755,190 speeches, every one having the carry of shrapnel" (Creel 1920).

After the end of World War I, the participants of the CPI's effort voiced concern about propaganda. George Creel published his account, How we Advertised America.

In it he critically evaluates the role of propaganda, recounting how Congress aimed to suppress its publication (1920).

During this time, widespread concern about the power of the new mass media developed. These fears were echoed among scientists, who assumed that mass media has extensive, direct, and powerful effects on attitude and behavior. The previously neutral term *propaganda* as a description of public persuasion acquired a negative connotation. Creel argued, "We did not call it propaganda. For that word, in German hands, had come to be associated with deceit and corruption. Our effort was educational and informative throughout, for we had such confidence in our case as to feel that no other argument was needed than the simple, straightforward presentation of facts." (1920)

Harold Lasswell posited in <u>Propaganda Technique in the World War</u> (1927) that the media could affect public opinion toward almost any point of view:

But when all allowances have been made, and all extravagant estimates pared to the bone, the fact remains that propaganda is one of the most powerful instrumentalities in the modern world. It has arisen to its present eminence in response to a complex of changed circumstances which have altered the nature of society... A newer and subtler instrument must weld thousands and even millions of human beings into one amalgamated mass of hate and will and hope. A new flame must burn out the canker of dissent and temper the steel of bellicose enthusiasm. The name of this new hammer and anvil of social solidarity is propaganda.

Lasswell affirms the power of propaganda, noting that the people had been deceived by propaganda during the war.[7]

Lasswell based his theory on a stimulus-response model rooted in learning theory. Stressing mass effects, his approach viewed human responses to the media as homogeneous and direct. This response, combined with the emerging concept of a mass society, thus created an environment susceptible to dangerous propaganda. The understanding of propaganda as a necessary evil of mass society is still influencing the discourse, playing a role in current critical media theory (Lazarsfeld 1957; Chomsky 1993).

Democratic Foreign Policy

At the same time, however, the regard of public diplomacy as democratic diplomacy entered the discourse. This view argued that the secret scheming of foreign policy elites had been responsible for the World War I and therefore a new open diplomacy was needed in order to avoid war. This open, or democratic, diplomacy was embodied in the first of Wilson's Fourteen Points of January 8, 1918, which outlined U.S. proposals for a peace settlement. Wilson demanded "[o]pen covenants of peace, openly arrived at, after which there shall be no private international under-

---

[7] For an overview of the literature, see: Harold Dwight Lasswell's, Propaganda and Promotional Activities, an annotated bibliography, prepared under the direction of the Advisory committee on pressure groups and propaganda, Social science research council (Lasswell 1935).

standings of any kind, but diplomacy shall proceed always frankly and in the public view."[8]

Open or public diplomacy was seen as a necessary complement to traditional government-to-government diplomacy. Two concepts were introduced that aimed to prevent wars caused by secret treaties: transparency and ratification. The first was a provision inserted as Article 18 in the Covenant of the League of Nations: "Every treaty or international engagement entered into hereafter by any member of the League shall be forthwith registered with the secretariat and shall as soon as possible be published by it. No such treaty or international engagement shall be binding until so registered."[9]

The second concept was an alteration of the practice of ratification. Ratification by elected bodies ensures the democratic participation in foreign policy and defeats secret treaties. The idea of open covenants is based on the Kantian concept of the republican peace, which requires republican or democratic domestic constitutions and a confederation of states in a system of international law (Kant 1995).[10] Wilson's idealism was not shared by others, however. He met opposition to his public diplomacy at the 1919 Paris Peace

---

[8] "Congressional Record, vol. 56 (1918), pt. 1, pp. 680-681." Reprinted in (Andrea, Overfield 1994, 384-386).

[9] The document can be accessed at: http://www.yale.edu/lawweb/avalon/leagcov.htm.

[10] "Es soll kein Friedensschluß für einen solchen gelten, der mit dem geheimen Vorbehalt des Stoffs zu einem künftigen Kriege gemacht worden." Quoted in Immanuel Kant: Zum ewigen Frieden. Ein philosophischer Entwurf (Kant 1995).

Conference, and the United States Senate rejected membership in the League, despite Wilson's extended speaking tour (Turner 1957). Consequently, the League did not succeed (Cooper 2001). However, the ideals of open diplomacy have since been integrated into successive international frameworks, such as the United Nations, and are accepted practice. This historic U.S. entry into public diplomacy, understood as propaganda on one hand and democratic diplomacy with the goal of achieving world peace on the other, lies at the heart of some of the contemporary debates about public diplomacy.

Exchange Programs

In the decades of the 1920s and early 1930s, interest for the conduct of American foreign policy in general was quite low. However, with the introduction of the first academic exchange programs, an important tool of public diplomacy was created (Ninkovich 1981). The 1936 Convention for the Promotion of Inter-American Cultural Relations provided an important thrust for the incorporation of cultural programs into U.S. diplomatic activity abroad. In 1938 the Department of State established the Division of Cultural Relations and an Interdepartmental Committee for Scientific Cooperation (Cherrington 1973). The idea behind exchange programs is that by experiencing American culture, visitors will be persuaded to think positively about the United States. Proponents of the exchange approach to public diplomacy argue that the complexity of the United States cannot be reduced to slogans and therefore only through the total immersion will participants of exchange programs achieve the necessary understanding of the United States (Tuch 1990).

Public Diplomacy as Counterpropaganda

Cordell Hull, U.S. Secretary of State from 1933 to 1944, focused on the promotion of cultural relations with Latin American nations, who were then supposedly targets for Nazi German propaganda. In 1940, President Roosevelt and Secretary of State Hull appointed Nelson Rockefeller to the post of Coordinator of Commercial and Cultural Affairs between the United States and Latin America. Rockefeller organized the first official International Visitor Program with trips by approximately forty Latin American leaders a year to the United States for 60-day tours. Programs and hospitality for most of the official visitors in major cities were organized by community organizations and university centers with a Latin American orientation. Over a period of several years, 128 journalists from 20 American republics made official visits in small groups to tour American cities and war industries. The analytical distinction between information and propaganda was introduced under the argument that the importance of information, rather than propaganda, was being stressed by scholars (Tuch 1990). American political elites viewed this program as an effective and successful balance against Nazi German propaganda in Central and South America (Espinosa 1976).[11]

Broadcasting Information

The invention of the radio made possible the real-time dissemination of information to a mass audience. As the United States entered World War II, Washington gave considerable attention to the organization of official governmental information and propaganda policy, argues Thomas

---

[11] National Archives and Records Administration: "Records of the Office of Inter-American Affairs" [OIAA] (Record Group 229) 1937-51.

C. Sorensen in <u>The Word War: The Story of American Propaganda</u> (1968). An Office of Facts and Figures was created in February 1942, along with the office of Coordinator of Information.[12] The Foreign Information Service was also established and a network of fourteen private short-wave transmitters began broadcasting the newly established Voice of America. Even today, many policy makers regard radio broadcasting as the most powerful tool of U.S. public diplomacy (Dizard 2001). The Middle East Radio Network and Radio Free Afghanistan, both instituted in 2002, exemplify this commitment.

Centralization vs. Decentralization

Centralizing information efforts in order to send a coherent message has been a reflex in situations of crisis since the days of the Creel Committee in World War I. During times of peace, these committees have been dismantled in order to avoid Orwellian totalitarianism, argues Allan Winkler in <u>The Politics of Propaganda: The Office of War Information, 1942-1945</u> (1978). In June of 1942, the Office of War Information (OWI) was established to consolidate distributed agencies of domestic and foreign information. By 1946, however, President Truman had terminated the OWI, placing the remainder within the State Department. In total, the

---

[12] <u>National Archives and Records Administration</u>: "Records of the Office of War Information" [OWI] (Record Group 208) 1926-51 (bulk 1941-46).

post World War II 11,000-strong personnel decreased to 3000, including Voice of America.

Within the State Department, the Office of International Information and Cultural Affairs (OIC) in 1946 had a network of 76 branches. Wireless files carried daily news and feature stories from Washington. Sixty-seven information centers and libraries stocked books, displayed exhibits and showed films. The Voice of America broadcasted to the world in 24 languages. In 1947, the OIC was renamed the Office of International Information and Educational Exchange to reflect its enlarged portfolio.[13]

At the end of the war, attention turned to building on wartime experience in information and international visitation. Authored by Senator J. William Fulbright of Arkansas, the Fulbright Act of 1946 established a peacetime international educational exchange program (Woods 1995).[14] The program was placed in the Department of State under the Office of International Information and Educational Exchange (OIE), administered by the Bureau of Public Affairs.[15] In time it increased to include 76 branches and officers abroad.

---

[13] National Archives and Records Administration: "Records of the United States Information Agency" [USIA] (Record Group 306)1900-88 (bulk 1947-86).

[14] Public Law 79-584.

[15] National Archives and Records Administration: "Records of the United States Information Agency" [USIA] (Record Group 306)1900-88 (bulk 1947-86).

Public Affairs vs. Public Diplomacy

As the Cold War started in 1947 and 1948, the Truman administration and Congress saw the need for a more significant U.S. role in world affairs. Paralleling the Truman Doctrine of 1947 and the Marshall Plan of 1948, which focused on the reconstruction of Europe and the use of development aid in order to challenge Soviet expansionism, the United States International Information and Educational Exchange Act of 1948 was passed as a measure to assure U.S.-friendly academic and political elites. Representative Karl E. Mundt and Senator H. Alexander Smith introduced the Act, establishing an official information agency for the first time in a period of peace.[16] The Smith-Mundt Act is also important because it posits that information produced for audiences outside the United States by the International Information Programs Office

> shall not be disseminated within the United States, its territories, or possessions, but, on request, shall be available in the English language at the Department of State, at all reasonable times following its release as information abroad, for examination only by representatives of United States press associations,

---

[16] <u>Smith-Mundt Act</u>. "The United States Information and Educational Exchange Act of 1948" 22 U.S.C. 1431, et seq.

56

newspapers, magazines, radio systems, and stations, and by research students and scholars, and, on request, shall be made available for examination only to Members of Congress.

This requirement thus officially distinguishes between the domestic public affairs and international public diplomacy. This distinction enables the government to pursue its goals internationally and to aggressively represent the interests of the U.S., while at the same time prohibiting the dissemination of strategic information on the inside, so that the democratic process was not endangered.

The Smith-Mundt Act also gives "full recognition to the importance of educational and cultural exchanges sponsored by the government...in recognition of the need to build up a corps of well-informed intellectuals and opinion leaders in the political and social infrastructure." Its goal is "to promote a better understanding of the United States in other countries, and to increase mutual understanding between Americans and foreigners."[17] Passed unanimously by Congress, the Act supplemented the 1946 Fulbright Act, becoming the basic document for postwar public diplomacy (Tuch 1990).

The separation between public affairs and public diplomacy that is necessary for a government to communicate strategically and speak for the nation in the international realm, yet keep the government from influencing its citizens domestically, has become problematic with the development of global media and the Internet.

---

[17] Public Law 82-402.

Anticommunism

Two bureaus were established at the Department of State to administer the Smith-Mundt Act: the Office of International Information for the media and the Office of Educational Exchanges for persons and libraries. The two were united in 1952 into a "semi-autonomous" agency at the State Department, the International Information Administration (IIA).[18] The IIA's semi-autonomous status reflected debate and concern about public diplomacy in the escalating Cold War. Some questioned whether exchange and information were sufficient to promote American interests in a divided world. Others feared that it would propagate strategic (dis)information domestically. It was quite clear, however, that the IIA was to operate exclusively abroad and not to disseminate information within the United States.

With the goal of creating groups of intellectuals and opinion leaders with close ties to the U.S., the International Visitor Program was started. It was launched with the German Reeducation Program, which was sponsored by the United States High Commissioner to Germany.[19]

---

[18] General Records of the Department of State (Record Group 59) 1756-1993.

[19] Records of the U.S. High Commissioner for Germany [USHCG] (Record Group 466).

Community Based Programs

Community-based nongovernmental organizations have also played a great role in the International Visitors Program.[20] These institutions argue that the objective of these exchanges was mutual learning by the visitors and the people with whom they came into contact. The emphasis was thus to be on information and education, not on propaganda. Similar to the long-term exchange programs, the visitor would then understand and appreciate American democracy and society with their specific characteristics and problems through information and education.

In 1948, seventy-nine West German leaders and specialists free of Nazi backgrounds were brought to the United States for extended visits. The purpose of the new Foreign Leader Program was to orient selected current and potential German leaders to American democracy and to engage in mutual exchanges with American people and institutions. The numbers increased to 557 in 1949 and approximately 2,500 in 1950. By the end of 2000, more than 100,000 International Visitors had traveled under the program, and 188 former International Visitors had achieved positions of

---

[20] http://www.nciv.org/, http://exchanges.state.gov/education/ivp/.

Chief of State or head of government in their home countries.[21]

Institutionalization: The United States Information Agency

In 1953, the Eisenhower administration, focusing on general government reorganization, decided to institutionalize public diplomacy. The newly established President's Advisory Commission on Governmental Reorganization, chaired by Nelson Rockefeller, the President's Committee on International Information Activities (the Jackson Committee), and the Senate's Special Subcommittee on Overseas Information Programs (the Hickenlooper Committee) focused on the issue (Gibson 1998). The main question under debate was whether information policy and exchanges should be managed by the Department of State, which has prime responsibility to formulate and execute U.S. foreign policy, or be granted autonomy. The Rockefeller Commission called on April 8, 1953, for an independent foreign information agency, whereas the Jackson and Hickenlooper committees recommended that the educational and cultural affairs programs be retained in the Department of State.[22] The Jackson Committee Report stated that,

---

[21] http://exchanges.state.gov/education/ivp/.

[22] Dwight D. Eisenhower Library Abilene, Kansas: "U.S. President's Advisory Committee on Government Organization:" Records, 1953-61 Acc. A67-3.

In reality, there is a "psychological" aspect or implication to every diplomatic, economic, or military policy and action. This implication should receive more careful attention, both in the planning and execution stage of policy . . . Every significant act of virtually every department and agency of Government has its effect, either positively or negatively, in the global struggle for freedom. The important task is to build awareness throughout the entire Government of the impact of day-to-day governmental actions and to coordinate and time such actions so as to derive from them the maximum advantages.[23]

The debates and differing views on this organizational confrontation were driven by special interests and the concern that public diplomacy programs might be too closely identified with the formulation and execution of U.S. foreign policy. A compromise to this debate established a new agency for information activities, but retained educational and cultural exchanges at the Department of State. As a result, Congressional Reorganization Plan Number 8 of June 1, 1953, called for the establishment of the United States Information Agency (USIA), which would absorb the activities of the State Department's International Information Administration (Malone 1988).[24] However, cultural and

---

[23] Dwight D. Eisenhower Library Abilene, Kansas: "U.S. President's Advisory Committee on International Information Activities(Jackson Committee):" Records, 1950-53Accession 83-9.

[24] Dwight D. Eisenhower Library Abilene, Kansas: "Morgan, Gerald D.: Records, 1953-61" Accessions: Pre-Acc., A67-57, and A67-19.

exchange programs remained under the Bureau of Public Affairs and the International Educational Exchange Service. USIA was formally established on August 1, 1953, with the Fulbright Act of 1946 and the Smith-Mundt Act of 1948 serving as its legislative base, until the Fulbright-Hayes Act of 1961 superseded the Fulbright and Smith-Mundt Acts (Gibson 1995). The Fulbright-Hayes Act aims to

> enable the Government of the United States to increase mutual understanding between the people of the United States and the people of other countries by means of educational and cultural exchange; to strengthen the ties which unite us with other nations by demonstrating the educational and cultural interests, developments, and achievements of the people of the United States and other nations, and the contributions being made toward a peaceful and more fruitful life for people throughout the world; to promote international cooperation for educational and cultural advancement; and thus to assist in the development of friendly, sympathetic, and peaceful relations between the United States and the other countries of the world. [25]

Specific mandates include, among other items, enabling exchange programs between scholars of various countries and the United States, creating American cultural centers and libraries, and participating in cultural exhibitions and

---

[25] Mutual Education and Cultural Exchange Act of 1961. Public Law 87-256.

fairs. The Bureau of Educational and Cultural Affairs oversaw these programs. USIA was designed to focus its programs, such as information and media operations, and its services, such as its libraries, exclusively on audiences abroad. Unlike the Creel Committee, the USIA was not tasked with conducting any information programs within the United States. Responsibility for cultural and educational exchanges eventually shifted from the State Department's Bureau of Public Affairs to a new Bureau of International Cultural Affairs, reflecting the increase in the volume and importance of cultural exchanges. USIA was given responsibility for operations abroad under the name of the United States Information Service (USIS), which operated under the umbrella and authority of U.S. embassies and consulates abroad (Tuch 1990).

Truth vs. Propaganda

In 1961, President John F. Kennedy appointed Edward R. Murrow to direct USIA and devoted considerable time and attention to the agency and to public diplomacy in general (Lichello 1971). At this time, the Bureau of Educational and Cultural Affairs at the State Department had five regional offices that paralleled those of USIA, the Agency for International Development (formerly the International Cooperation Administration), and the Peace Corps. The passage of the Fulbright-Hayes Act in 1961 underlined the objective of increasing mutual understanding between the people of the

United States and the peoples of other nations. The focus during this time was on conceptualizing public diplomacy as information, not as propaganda. Edward R. Murrow testified in May 1963 before a Congressional Committee, "American traditions and the American ethic require us to be truthful, but the most important reason is that truth is the best propaganda and lies are the worst. To be persuasive we must be believable; to be believable we must be credible; to be credible we must be truthful. It is as simple as that."(Brown 2002)

Realpolitik and Other Critics

In some ways, public diplomacy received inflated expectations during the Kennedy administration. In this period of the Cold War, public diplomacy seemed to offer the West an offensive strategic option that was otherwise lacking because of the nuclear balance of terror. Yet the difficulty of bringing about near-term change in the closed societies of the East was initially underestimated, while the efficacy of propaganda as a political tool was overrated. On the other hand, public diplomacy was an unsure instrument of foreign policy. When the Soviet army quenched the Radio Free Europe-encouraged Hungarian revolution of 1956, official thinking in the West began to take a more reserved stance toward its claims of efficacy as is argued by Walter L. Hixson in <u>Parting the Curtain: Propaganda, Culture and the Cold War</u> (1977). With the American involvement in Vietnam, the idea that the hearts and minds of the world's masses could be won came to seem problematic. The term "winning the hearts and minds" was coined by the Lyndon B. Johnson administration to express the need to win over the population in the villages in Vietnam.[26] In essence, the belief in the infallibility of American exceptionalism was damaged.

In the aftermath of the Vietnam War, the traditional programs and assumptions of Cold War public diplomacy faced a serious challenge from within the policy elite itself. CIA sponsorship of Radio Free Europe/Radio Liberty was exposed in the U.S. Senate in 1971. According to Frances Stonor Saunders in Who Paid the Piper?: The CIA and the Cultural Cold War (1999), the radios were reconstituted as a private corporation under oversight arrangements of a new Board for International Broadcasting (BIB) that was supposed to serve as a firewall against direct government propaganda but clandestine sponsorship continued. The rationale was that broadcasting should be independent in order to be trustworthy, though remained focused on furthering the U.S. interest in general.[27]

After a Vietnam-era decline, the Carter administration renewed attention to the infrastructure of public diplomacy. A 1977 plan for restructuring public diplomacy led to the creation of a new agency, the U.S. International Communication Agency (USICA), formally established on April 1, 1978 (Snow 1997). USICA was a merger of the

---

[26] http://www.pbs.org/newshour/bb/media/july-dec01/heartsminds_11-1.html.
[27] http://www.ibb.gov/bbg/.

USIA and the Department of State's Division of Educational and Cultural Affairs. The new agency received responsibility for nearly all official exchange and visitor programs. Ambassador John E. Reinhardt, director of USIA, became the first director of USICA and reported to the President and the Secretary of State.

This renewed focus on public diplomacy was encouraged by new developments in the Cold War. Soviet endorsement of the human rights provisions of the Helsinki Final Act in 1975 unexpectedly stimulated dissident activity in the Soviet bloc and elevated the international profile of human rights violations by governments everywhere (Hixson 1976). The Carter administration made human rights a central concern of American foreign policy, and in the process set out to rehabilitate public diplomacy as a legitimate activity of the U.S. government (Tuch 1990).

In 1978, the Department of State ended its association with educational and cultural exchanges, giving control to USICA. Some welcomed the move of the administration and operations of exchange programs from State to the independent new agency, believing that it would lessen those programs' association with the more direct political aspects of U.S. foreign policy. Others, such as Senator Fulbright, who had always demanded that the exchange programs be located at the State Department, disagreed.

Military Strength and Moral Clarity

Ronald Reagan, who often is presented as having an ultra-realist perspective in foreign affairs, had a strong belief in the effectiveness of public diplomacy. Many viewed his definition of public diplomacy, however, as propaganda. Reagan's interest in public diplomacy logically originated from his personal background as an actor and his skills as a communicator (Ryan 2001). On October 14, 1982, he signed Executive Order 12388, restoring the USIA name to the agency and reviving USIS as the name of its operations abroad.[28]

Reagan's choice for director of USIA was Charles Z. Wick (Laurien 1988). Through his personal access to the president, he was able to increase the stature of USIA. His approach was based on what Neoconservatives today call "military strength and moral clarity".[29] By mid-1982, the administration had developed the outlines of an international communication strategy. The National Security Decision Directive (NSDD) 45 affirmed that international broadcasting constitutes a major instrument of U.S. national security policy and stated that improvement in programming as well as the technical quality of U.S. broadcasting are requirements of the highest priority. It directed the Voice of America to strengthen existing mechanisms for relating program content to current U.S. foreign and national security policy objectives, and to ensure that commentary and analysis incorporated vigorous advocacy of

[28] http://www.reagan.utexas.edu/resource/speeches/1982/101482e.htm.
[29] the website of the Organization for a new American Century gives a good picture of this perspective: www.newamericancentury.org.

current U.S. policy positions. [30] It also focused attention on the role of American international broadcasting in times of crisis and war, and called on the relevant agencies to review existing guidance and make recommendations for closer integration of the broadcasting effort into political and military contingency planning. The NSSD 45 exemplifies a return to the propagandistic approach to public diplomacy that had marked the early years of the Cold War (Tuch 1990). The National Security Decision Directive 130 of 1984 addressed only the information component of public diplomacy, yet the principles laid in this directive down had greater relevance than in previous measures. [31] It noted that public diplomacy is "a key strategic instrument for shaping fundamental political and ideological trends around the globe on a long-term basis and ultimately affecting the behavior of governments.

In an effort to counter the tendency of viewing public diplomacy as neutral information, the NSDD made clear that the fundamental purpose of international information programs is to affect foreign audiences in ways favorable to U.S. national interests, and stressed that "the habits, interests, expectations and level of understanding of foreign audiences may differ significantly from those of the domestic American audience, and require different approaches and emphases in the selection and presentation of information." [32]

---

[30] http://www.fas.org/irp/offdocs/nsdd/nsdd-045.htm.

[31] http://www.fas.org/irp/offdocs/nsdd/nsdd-130.htm.

[32] http://www.fas.org/irp/offdocs/nsdd/23-2213t.gif.

At the same time, the document made clear that public diplomacy programs should be understood as a strategic instrument of U.S. national policy, not a tactical instrument of U.S. diplomacy, and hence should not be surrendered to the need of improving government-to-government relations with particular countries. Reflecting this strategic perspective, the NSDD emphasized the potential contributions of the Department of Defense in the information field, and called for the revitalization of psychological operations (PSYOP) within the U.S. military establishment as well as coordinated information planning across all affected agencies.

Information Technology

When Reagan took office in 1981, the broadcasting technology used by the Voice of America dated from World War II. The combination of a relatively weak signal and heavy jamming sharply limited its audience in the Soviet Union, especially in major cities and the non-Russian republics. A Ronald Reagan-sponsored technical modernization program created the infrastructure for a strengthened international broadcasting effort. The launching of Radio Marti, broadcasting to Cuba, was another major public diplomacy initiative undertaken early in the administration. In spite of fierce opposition from the National Association of Broadcasters, which feared Cuban retaliation against U.S. commercial broadcasters, Congress passed legislation for the implementation Radio Marti in 1983. Later that year, USIA introduced WORLDNET, a global television satellite broadcast that allowed direct access to foreign television

audiences. Interactive video conferences with foreign journalists were the main use of this medium. USIA also began
to use the medium wave radio band, hoping to broaden its
audience, particularly among younger generations.

Democratizing the World

In 1983 the National Endowment for Democracy (NED)
was established to serve as the primary vehicle for supporting democratic development abroad. Relying on the Wilsonian argument of peace through democratization, the
NED started a trend that has developed into a democratization industry with revenues of several $100 million in 1999
(Carother 1999). The NED is a private, nonprofit organization created to strengthen democratic institutions around
the world through nongovernmental efforts. It is governed
by an independent, nonpartisan board of directors. With its
annual congressional appropriations, it funds hundreds of
grants each year to support pro-democracy groups in Africa, Asia, Central and Eastern Europe, Latin America, the
Middle East, and the former Soviet Union. It is exemplary
for a new ideology loosely based on the democratic peace
paradigm in international relations, arguing that by aiding
states to develop democratic institutions, the world can be
made a safer place. Over time, a industry of democratizers
has developed, now involving many government agencies
from the Pentagon to the USAID(Carothers 1999).[33]

---

[33] see for example: www.marshallcenter.org.

Post Cold War Politics: Integrating USIA into State

As the primary aim and legitimization of USIA had been to undermine support for communism worldwide, the end of the Cold War led to a debate about the agency's role in future foreign policy. With the end of history eminent (Fukuyama 1992), it seemed that the USIA might no long be necessary. In 1990 USIA's Oversight Commission On Public Diplomacy criticized its disappointedly slow response to the newest developments in Eastern Europe. The George H.W. Bush administration budget of 1991 did not provide enough funds for USIA, requiring cutbacks in its programs. The debates over the future strategy of public diplomacy in 1993 and 1994 focused mostly on TV Marti, the needs for a new Radio Free Asia, the relationship of USIA to Radio Free Europe and Radio Liberty, and the number of languages broadcast by Voice of America. The most accurate description of these discussions would be bureaucratic inertia and puzzlement over the State Department's role in the new world order, according to the CSIS study <u>Reinventing Diplomacy in the Information Age Center for Strategic and International Studies</u> (2000).

Behind these debates stood special interests. For example, due to technical problems and treaty obligations, TV Marti only broadcast between 3:30 and 6:00 A.M.; moreover it was jammed by the Cuban government. The broadcast only continued due to vested interests by the Cuban-American Miami constituency. Furthermore, Radio Free Europe and Radio Liberty had problems both with former

CIA agents that were still working there and no clear-cut mission for the institutions.

The Clinton administration again had a different approach to public diplomacy. On April 17, 1997, President Bill Clinton approved a broad reorganization of the Department of State, which called for the USIA along with the Arms Control and Disarmament Agency to be incorporated into the State Department, thus losing their autonomy and independence as foreign policy agencies.[34] Chairman of the Senate Foreign Relations Committee Jesse Helms, who had long demanded a reorganization of the nation's foreign policy bureaucracy, advocated this consolidation. Vice President Al Gore's Reinventing Government program had included several years of similar proposals for streamlining the foreign policy structures (Gore 2001).

Two major studies of strategic nature in the 1990s examined U.S. public diplomacy: the Stimson Center (2000) and the Center for Strategic and International Studies (2000). The Omnibus Reconciliation Bill, passed in October 1998, called for the reorganization of U.S. foreign affairs agencies, a long-discussed and much-debated move that merged both the U.S. Information Agency (USIA) and the Arms Control and Disarmament Agency (ACDA) into the U.S. Department of State. The Foreign Affairs Reform and Restructuring Act of 1998 mandated the integration of

---

[34] "Reorganization Plan and Report Submitted by President Clinton to the Congress on December 30, 1998, Pursuant to Section 1601 of the Foreign Affairs Reform and Restructuring Act of 1998," as contained in Public Law 105-277.

USIA into the State Department to be completed by Oct. 1, 1999. This in theory signified a major shift towards placing public diplomacy as a centerpiece of U.S. foreign policy. However, different bureaucratic cultures prevented this integration from becoming successful.

Conclusion

The chapter has shown that different understandings of public diplomacy have led to different policy outcomes. By describing its historical foundations can one better understand the contemporary discourse on public diplomacy. History in the policy area of public diplomacy can be described as a catwalk showing of arguments and ideas. In the Bush administration's discourse on public diplomacy post September 11, many of the historic arguments again play a role. However, we do not yet know why, when, and how these arguments will be used and what is different about the world we live in today—in essence, we understand something, but not enough.

The Political Significance of Base Metaphors in International Relations

In chapter three, I analyze the conceptual foundations of international relations and how they impact our ability to ascribe meaning to foreign policy instruments such as public diplomacy. The question driving this chapter is to find out how base metaphors shape the practice of international relations, in order to uncover and recover the political questions that need to be addressed before we can even talk about communicating foreign policy. I argue that a shift is taking place from the metaphor of the international system as a Hobbesian state of nature to an Aristotelian language community.

Das Erkennen ist nur ein Arbeiten in den beliebtesten Meta-
phern.
(Nietzsche 1999)

As in manufacture so in science – retooling is an extravagance to
be reserved for the occasion that demands it. The significance of
crises is the indication they provide that an occasion for retooling
has arrived.
(Kuhn 1970)

Crisis: Revisiting the First Problem From Chapter 1

In the last chapter, I argued en passant that the discipline of
international relations has not developed a mature discourse on communicating foreign policy. I blamed this on
the base metaphor of the discipline, the Hobbesian state of
nature, which is unable to address questions about language, persuasion, communication and community. However, the global governance discourse and its underlying
base metaphors of the network or the communicative realm
proffer a serious challenge to this understanding. Because
of the tectonic nature of this possible shift in base metaphors and the interdependence between theory and ab-

stract policy making, it is necessary to take a closer look at this issue and unearth the discipline's politics of base metaphors. A shared understanding of international relations as a communicative realm will have an influence on how public diplomacy is perceived.

This has to be done carefully, because the vocabulary to deal with this type of critical inquiry has not been introduced to international relations and the base metaphor of the Hobbesian state of nature is more deeply entrenched than we often realize. The Hobbesian state of nature has a dual function in the discipline: on one hand it delineates international relations as the outside to the inside of political theory, thereby legitimating it as a self-sustaining but complementary academic field (Walker 1993); on the other hand, it excludes communication and community, thus achieving natural science status, which again increases legitimacy (Waltz 1979). Any critical perspective on the base metaphors of the discipline will therefore delegitimize and (re)politicize the issue, which is painful because if taken seriously, it undermines professionalization efforts and cumulative projects.

Therefore, the question driving this chapter is to find out what base metaphors do and how they shape the practice of international relations, in order to unearth the political questions that need to be addressed before we can discuss public diplomacy.

My argument involves three steps. First, I aim to show that it is impossible to base any discipline on anything but metaphorical imagery. Then I argue that in international relations, the interdependence between theory and policy forces us to focus on how they interact in any general argument. In the third step, I ask what is happening in international relations, and because of steps one and two, make the argument that the choice of a base metaphor is political. Therefore, because we have no possibility to reduce questions of base metaphor choice to questions that can be answered by referring to scientific validity, and because these questions matter, we need to delineate the politics of base metaphors in the discipline of international relations.

Background

International relations is a unique field for several reasons. As in all social realms, truth is dependent on its objects of analysis: what policy makers think is true becomes the truth-- if they act upon it. International relations it is a very small discipline both on the policy and theory levels, allowing individuals to play a large role in imagining the truth of theory and policy. International policy making is an abstract practice, especially in contrast to local politics. We reify and anthropomorphize corporate actors, such as states and supranational organizations, and consequently our expectations about appropriate behavior are very much dependent on what characteristics we ascribe to these 'non-natural' persons. If, however, this means that initial choices about how we conceptualize international relations matters in the real world, both at the theoretical and policy levels, the choice of a base metaphor delineating the discipline of international relations becomes political.

Furthermore, if this choice is political, it has to be brought out into the open to debunk the arguments of actors in the theory and policy discourses that argue their approach is more legitimate because it is more scientific or more 'natural.' In order to deal with this type of problem, I take the vocabulary of the philosophy of science to describe a process that is taking place in international relations.

This is an interesting project for three reasons. There is a *crisis*, or uncertainty about the validity of the dominant paradigm, in international relations that manifests itself as a battle on many levels of abstraction and substance. I argue that a base metaphor approach can consolidate these individual skirmishes into one main battlefield. Especially since September 11, we have seen that international relations and our images of the international realm are being debated vigorously (Walt 2001; Hirsch 2002).

This crisis has manifested itself both on the policy and the theory levels. On the policy level, a shift of focus can be observed from counting nuclear warheads to questions of bandwidth requirements, transnational criminal networks, globalization, and terrorism. The mainstream explanations for this shift are globalization, the end of the Cold War, and September 11.

On the theory level, the discipline of international relations is involved in a major epistemological debate between a natural science positivism and post-positivism, where questions of identity are raised (Zalewski 1996).

This debate has been going on for some time and is only partially related to globalization and the demise of Cold War thinking (Lapid 1989). Mark Neufeld has taken the debate to the meta-theoretical level with his <u>Restructuring of International Relations Theory</u> (1995) introducing critical perspectives on the epistemological level. On the surface, these crises are different. They are derived from a historical context, i.e. globalization and the end of the Cold War, and a theoretical context, i.e. the clashes between positivism and post-positivism (Wendt 1999).

I will argue that to understand both crises we need to go below the surface of the debates and focus on the foundation level of the discipline. Both the theory and practice of international relations share basic assumptions about what constitutes the international system; this sharing, in turn, reinforces the assumptions. In the mainstream discourse, the *international system* is defined as the non-national, non-hierarchical anarchic realm. R. B. J. Walker (1993, 171) argues,

> Relations between states are conventionally understood as the negation of the community presumed to be possible within the sovereign state. Whether characterized as politics without centralized authority, as an international anarchy, or as a more or less mechanical (automatic rather than political) system, international relations is defined both by the presence of sovereign states as primary actors and by the absence of a sovereign power/authority governing the system itself.

Behind this most basic foundational understanding lies the metaphor of conceptualizing the international realm as a Hobbesian state of nature as is argued by Beate Jahn in <u>The</u>

Cultural Construction of International Relations : The Invention of the State of Nature (2000). This understanding has recently come under attack. In order to understand this challenge, we need to focus on the most basic concepts of the discipline, problematize them, expose the imagery they are based upon, and offer alternative images. This means that we need to address the grammar of our concepts. We ask questions such as, "How do we use a concept and what does this imply?" By focusing on the normally unquestioned base metaphor and the questions this type of inquiry enables us to ask, we can expose the politics behind discursive moves and provide a clearer perspective on important issues.

What Do Metaphors Do? Pushing Back the Envelope on Intuition

All scientific disciplines rely on intuition as the last reason for why one sees the world one way and not another. Aristotle has stated this quite clearly in Nicomachean Ethics (1984, book VI, chapter 6):

> Scientific knowledge is judgment about things that are universal and necessary, and the conclusions of demonstration, and all scientific knowledge, follow from first principles (for scientific knowledge involves apprehension of a rational ground). This being so, the first principle from which what is scien-

tifically known follows cannot be an object of scientific knowledge, of art, or of practical wisdom; for that which can be scientifically known can be demonstrated, and art and practical wisdom deal with things that are variable. Nor are these first principles the objects of philosophic wisdom, for it is a mark of the philosopher to have demonstration about some things. If, then, the states of mind by which we have truth and are never deceived about things invariable or even variable are scientific knowledge, practical wisdom, philosophic wisdom, and intuitive reason, and it cannot be any of the three (i.e. practical wisdom, scientific knowledge, or philosophic wisdom), the remaining alternative is that it is intuitive reason that grasps the first principles.

We can push back the envelope a little further if we introduce the concept of base metaphors that allow us to rationalize this first intuition in metaphorical relations. Base metaphors can describe what persuades adherents of paradigms of their fruitfulness. In times of transformative change, during which how we imagine the world is up for grabs, this is where politics takes place. Therefore, the concept of base metaphors offers great explanatory leverage relating to the recent developments in international relations.

A metaphor is the use of a familiar image to illuminate an unfamiliar idea, experience, or process (Fauconnier 1997). It is a figure of speech that implies comparison between two unlike entities, as distinguished from the explicit comparison of a simile. The metaphor makes a qualitative leap from a reasonable image to an identification or fusion of two objects in order to make one new entity featuring characteristics of both. Analogies are a special case of metaphors insofar that analogies are relational, or, as Aristotle writes, proportional. George Lakoff and Mark Johnson (1980) argue that metaphors facilitate thought by providing a framework in which newly acquired, abstract concepts can be accommodated. The network of metaphors that underlie thought form a cognitive map, a web of concepts organized in terms which serves to ground abstract concepts in the cognitive agent's physical experiences, and in the agent's relation to the external world. Researchers such as George Lakoff, Mark Johnson, and Gilles Fauconnier argue that all of our thinking relies on images, metaphors, similes, myths, analogies, etc (Lakoff, Johnson 1980, 1999). Gilles Fauconnier argues (1997),

Our conceptual networks are intricately structured by analogical and metaphorical mappings, which play a key role in the synchronic construction of meaning in its diachronic evolution. Parts of such mappings are so entrenched in everyday thought and language that we do not consciously notice them; other parts strike us as novel and creative. The term metaphor is often applied to the latter, highlighting the literary and poetic aspects of the phenomenon. But the general cognitive principles at work are the same, and they play a key role in thought and language at all levels.

I will rely on the vocabulary and argumentative moves made in Hans Blumenberg's <u>Paradigmen zu einer Metaphorologie</u> in order to understand the crises in the discipline of international relations (1999). I will also draw on concepts and vocabulary introduced by Thomas Kuhn in his <u>Structure of Scientific Revolutions</u> (1970). Directly applying Thomas Kuhn's paradigms to the social sciences is problematic; however, they can be applied carefully and analogously.

I describe base metaphors as foundational for a way of thinking about international relations. Base metaphors are rhetoric figures that rely on imagery in order to legitimize specific ways of seeing a field of inquiry that cannot be corroborated through further rationalization: they are *uncausal first movers*. Base metaphors seem intuitively plausible to the community that subscribes to them and are normally experienced as unproblematic background knowledge and are stable over time.

During times of stability, or in Kuhnian terms *normal science*, base metaphors are not the focus of research. However, persisting anomalies and disturbances within a field lead to a general questioning of base assumptions of a discipline (Waismann 1968). This, in turn, leads to a general anxiety and crisis in the discipline. The anxiety generated in such crises is often not understood by scholars, who do not focus on base metaphors. Problematic base metaphors are more difficult to deal with than problematic theorems, because their conceptual power to evoke images with inherent plausibility.

It is necessary to clarify the vocabulary of base metaphors. The *base metaphor* is an improvable image that seems to be intuitively plausible to the members of a community subscribing to it and thus structures their world. A *discipline* can be referred to as a loose community of theorists and policy makers sharing interests in ontology, epistemology and practice of international relations. This definition relates to Thomas Kuhn's definition of *paradigms*: models of accepted scientific practice, consisting of laws, theory, applications, and instrumentation (Kuhn 10). Paradigms comprise a body of axioms and theorems both explicitly stated and implied that are derived from or informed by the base metaphor and shared by a community.

It is therefore necessary to focus on the *recursive relationship* between theory and policy in international relations. In fact, this focus is more important in this field than in other social sciences, because the policy of international relations is an abstract practice, where decisions taken today will have repercussions not limited by time and distance. Additionally, these important decisions are not directly accessible to the policy maker, and a very small, interested elite exerts great power over distributional decisions. Consider, for example, the impact that Wohlstetter's (1958) writings on balance of terror have had on the allocation of funds for nuclear capabilities, both in the U.S. and the U.S.S.R., or Kennan's X-article in <u>Foreign Affairs</u> (1947) on U.S. foreign policy in general.

In order to evaluate a crisis on the level of base metaphors, the following questions need to be addressed: What is the role of base metaphors for a discipline? What is the foundational base metaphor in international relations and with which scenarios can it be used? What alternative metaphors are being offered and which scenarios can it deal with and which not? What will be future developments of the discipline?

What is the Role of Base Metaphors for a Discipline?

The idea that disciplines rely on metaphorical is connected closely to Hans Blumenberg's body of work. In <u>Paradigmen einer Metaphorologie</u> (1999), he focuses on metaphors that have played formative roles in the history of mankind. Blumenberg defines *metaphorology* as a component of the history of ideas. He then argues that metaphors are as real as ideas, referring to them as *absolute metaphors*. Examples he uses are the clockwork metaphor of Newtonian physics and the light metaphor for truth in Aristotelian thought.

Blumenberg argues that metaphors are not verifiable; therefore, metaphorology does not test anything. However, the question of the truthfulness of metaphors is not irrelevant. He argues that the truth of absolute metaphors is in a very broad sense pragmatic.

Accepting that there are no final explanations for the reasons and nature of our actions means that the field must open to politics. The evaluation of base metaphors that form the foundation of a discipline is not a neutral undertaking that can be resolved by applying criteria of validity of scientific inquiry (Maturana 1992, 34). Following Thomas Kuhn, it entails a political act, or a phase of revolutionary science. "The act of judgment that leads scientists to reject a previously accepted theory is always based upon more than a comparison of that theory with the world. The decision to reject one paradigm is always simultaneously the decision to accept another, and the judgment leading to that decision involves the comparison of both paradigms with nature and with each other" (Kuhn 1970, 77). It entails an act of arguing, persuading, and coalition-building that exceeds the neutral realm of the scientific discourse. Kuhn argues (94),

> [l]ike the choice between competing political institutions, that between competing paradigms proves to be a choice between incompatible modes of community life. Because it has that character, the choice is not and cannot be determined merely by the evaluative procedures characteristic of normal science, for these depend in part upon a particular paradigm, and that paradigm is at issue.

The choice for one foundational metaphor over an other for a discipline is a value choice, and is therefore political in nature. In Kuhn's words (94),

> When paradigms enter, as they must, into a debate about paradigm choice, their role is necessarily circular. Each group uses its own paradigm to argue in that paradigm's defense. The resulting circularity does not, of course, make the arguments wrong or even ineffectual. The man who premises a paradigm when arguing in its defense can nonetheless provide

a clear exhibit of what scientific practice will be like for those who adopt the new view of nature.

The decision for one paradigm over another can never be made through the reliance on scientific criteria of validity. Hans Blumenberg uses the image of an astronaut who, even though she has the outer space perspective on the world, cannot validate the base metaphor of a paradigm, because she cannot leave the paradigm of macro-level physics: "Aber die Metapher hat es eben nicht mit theoretisch verifizierbaren – etwa astronautisch nachprüfbaren – Problemen zu tun; sie will mehr wissen, als je ein Astronaut wird feststellen können." (155) It is indeed a political act, involving argument and persuasion. Thomas Kuhn argues (94),

> yet, whatever its force, the status of the circular argument is only that of persuasion. It cannot be made logically or even probabilistically compelling for those who refuse to step into the circle. The premises and values shared by the two parties to a debate over paradigms are not sufficiently extensive for that. As in political revolutions, so in paradigm choice – there is no standard higher than the assent of the relevant community.

This pushing back the envelope on Aristotle's intuition is necessary in times of transformative change to unearth the politics that is taking place on this level.

What Differentiates the Natural from the Social?

Thomas Kuhn's Structure of Scientific Revolutions, which focuses on the natural sciences, opens the debate of whether one should use his method to analyze the social sciences. He contends that it is unclear what parts of social science have yet acquired such paradigms at all (Kuhn 15). Furthermore, once can easily argue that in international relations, no consensus on one base metaphor exists, so that the type of inquiry I am suggesting is not relevant to the discipline. However, if not full paradigms, which, defined by Kuhn, are models of accepted scientific practice, consisting of laws, theory, applications, and instrumentation (Kuhn 10), disciplines in the social sciences share base metaphors and accepted practices that function in a way analogous to Kuhnian paradigms. Even though the state of nature base metaphor has never been left uncontested in international relations, it is so deeply ingrained that it has had great impact on both the theoretical and policy discourses, as can be seen in the writings of such journals as International Organization, World Politics, International Security and at the policy level in Foreign Affairs and Foreign Policy.[35] It is important to recognize that even in the

---

[35] Think of: John Mearsheimers'. "The False Promise of International Institutions." International Security 19:3 (Winter 1994/95), pp. 5-49. See also responses in International Security 20:1. Summer 1995, pp. 39-93, Robert Jervis' "Cooperation Under the Security Dilemma." World Politics 30:2. January 1978, pp. 167-214., Thomas J. Christensen and Jack Snyders', "Chain Gangs and Passed Bucks: Predicting Alliance Patterns in Multipolarity." International Organization 44:2. Spring 1990, pp. 137-

natural sciences there is never a total adherence to one paradigm at a specific point in time (Feyerabend 1991).

Base metaphors in the social realm often have remained relatively stable over time. For example, in political theory the metaphor of society as a body was foundational from antiquity to the 17th century, and still influences our thinking today. The body politic metaphor is expressed most prominently in Livy's Speech of Menenius Agrippa (Livy 1998). The social contract metaphor has shaped the debate since then from Hobbes (1998) to Rawls (1971). In both these instances the base metaphor has been with us for longer than important paradigms in the natural sciences, such as either the Newtonian (1953) or the Einsteinian (1952) paradigms. The appeal of a specific base metaphor has great impact on the relevance of a discipline in the culture of the academy. It seems very questionable that the discipline of economics would be as successful as it is today if its base metaphor were not the marketplace, a colorful and friendly metaphor for exchange relations, but rather the prisoners' dilemma, a metaphor that describes exactly the same situation. It could be argued that neo-classical economics, with its focus on the self-regulating aspects of markets and the disinterest in designing the institution of the market for the greater good of an external public, is unwittingly moving from the marketplace metaphor to the

---

168, Ernst B. Haas', "The Balance of Power: Prescription, Concept, or Propaganda?" World Politics 5:4. July 1953, pp. 442-477, or Wolfgang H. Reinickes', „Global Public Policy," in Foreign Affairs November/December, 1997.

prisoners' dilemma metaphor. Fundamental critics of neo-liberal globalization definitely refer to this when voicing their criticism (e.g. Klein 1999).

These examples show how base metaphors structure our understanding of the world and that their truth is pragmatic (Blumenberg 1998, 25).

> Ihre Wahrheit ist, in einem sehr weiten Verstande, pragmatisch. Ihr Gehalt bestimmt als Anhalt von O-rientierungen ein Verhalten, sie geben einer Welt Struktur, repräsentieren das nie erfahrbare, nie über-sehbare Ganze der Realität. Dem historisch verste-henden Blick indizieren sie also die fundamentalen, tragenden Gewissheiten, Vermutungen, Wertungen, aus denen sich die Haltungen, Erwartungen, Tätig-keiten und Untätigkeiten, Sehnsüchte und Enttäu-schungen, Interessen und Gleichgültigkeiten einer Epoche regulierten.

However, even if base metaphors in social sciences are similar to the natural sciences' paradigms, an important constitutive difference exists: The recursive relationship between theory and policy. The social world is imagined by its 'objects of analysis' and how it is imagined can change. In social sciences, the objects of analyses are actors that are, in principle, able to reflect on their situation, base decisions on these reflections, and are able to imagine themselves as parts of collectivities. In order to make these decisions, they must conceptualize their environment. In turn, these concepts are interdependent with concepts on the theory level. Terms we use when talking about this theory-policy relationship are that of self-fulfilling prophecies, politics of ideas, pundits, the influence of think tanks on Washington politics, etc. Steve Smith argues (13),

> International theory underpins and informs international practice, even if there is a lengthy lag between the high-point of theories and their gradual absorption into political debate. Once established as common sense, theories become incredibly powerful since they delineate not simply what can be known but also what it is sensible to talk about or suggest. [...] Theories do not simply explain or predict, they tell us what possibilities exist for human action and intervention; they define not merely our explanatory possibilities but also our ethical and practical horizons.

Therefore, as long as a critical number of actors believes in the plausibility of a theory, it will be corroborated by future events, thereby becoming a self-fulfilling prophecy (Watzlawick 1984). Such self-fulfilling mechanisms can lead to quite stable paradigms, such as the gold standard in the 19th century, or to very unstable paradigms, such as the "new economy" of 1999/2000. Self-reinforcing mechanisms follow a different logic than linear causal mechanisms, insofar that their behavior can best be described with the metaphorical vocabulary of complexity theory, such as tipping points, self-sustaining equilibrium, and unintended consequences (Jervis 1997; Gladwell 2000).

By using the vocabulary of complexity theory and their base metaphors, such as Bikes-in-Beijing, Butterflies, and

Coastlines-from-Space (Gleick 1987), we can potentially save our scientific outlook and model the interdependency between theory and policy (Cedermann 1997; Axelrod 1997). However, by relying on such descriptions, we choose to ignore that in social systems the drivers of the self-reproducing phenomena are policy makers, reflexive actors able to imagine their worlds and collectivity. Recursive phenomena in social systems are therefore per definition different from recursive phenomena in complexity theory, which should not be surprising, because we assumed it ex ante. Or put tautologically, if we want to differentiate between the terms 'social' and 'natural,' we have to ascribe freedom to actors, which means that to a certain extent all truth is political in the social realm, which is the same as saying that our theories need to be able to deal with freedom.

Therefore, we need a framework to describe and explain what is happening on the level where actors use the vocabulary of science to legitimize political claims. By exposing the politics on this level, we can empower their principals to demand better explanations for their decisions and actions. Lord John Maynard Keynes makes this type of argument in <u>General Theory of Employment, Interest and Money</u> (1936). He argues: "Practical men, who believe themselves to be quite exempt from any intellectual influences, are usually the slaves of some defunct economist,"

Conceptualizing this recursive relationship between theory and policy is difficult but not impossible. As a first approach we can sketch it as politics on two levels:[36] the theory level and policy level. The theory level is where the abstract subject of international relations is described, explained, and predicted, whereas on the policy level the international realm is imagined and (re)produced through acts by policy makers.

Politics on the theory level is similar to Kuhn's revolutionary science in that different paradigms compete for dominance. Although the policy level has no counterpart in the Kuhnian model, it can easily be integrated: As long as policy makers believe that they are living in a Hobbesian state of nature, no paradigmatic change on the theory level would make sense.

Therefore, one has to be very careful not to confuse the two levels and not to conclude from a correspondence of behavior on the policy level with the expectations of the theory level that one's theory has been once and for all corroborated. It might also mean that the scholars had been able to persuade the actor to act, or the actor has persuaded the scholar that his actions derive of causal necessity and not personal idiosyncrasy, or the scholar and the policy maker have both gone to the same prep school. This makes any inquiry difficult, yet interesting, and the distinction between theory and policy levels necessary.

---

[36] These levels are epistemological constructs, not ontological givens.

What is the Mainstream Base Metaphor in International Relations and What does it do to the Discipline?

The mainstream base metaphor of international relations has been the Hobbesian state of nature, operationalized as anarchy, or more precisely as anomy (Waltz 1979). By delineating the inside (the hierarchy of the nation state) from the outside (the anomic realm of relations between equal nation states), international relations thinkers could infer a different logic of coaction, thus creating a new discipline (Walker 1993, Jahn 2000). While political theory inside the state dealt with the achievement of the good life, survival in the international realm was assured by balancing capabilities. While political theory had to deal with non clear-cut normative issues, international relations was able to rely on a clean "natural science" approach because actors' choice in the international system was so restrained by the anarchy of the system that it could be excluded, similar to how we do not have to focus on the individual choice of a seller to set her own price in a perfectly competitive market (Waltz 1979; Keohane 1986; Baldwin 1993). It has never been the only image shaping international relations, though it has been seminal in the mainstream discourse.

The anarchy-hierarchy dichotomy has taken the politics out of theorizing about social relations. The realist reading of it as an anomy-tyranny dichotomy, delineating the national, where a government provides security and enables the differentiation of functions, from the international level, where self-sufficient states interact in a self-help system, has come at a price. It is a simplification for reasons of theoretical coherence and predictive power. In its simplicity it is very convincing and powerful intuition because it seems like a lowest common denominator for any discourse. The problem is that it is so deprived of anything substantial that nothing can be deduced from it. However, this does not keep realists from claiming that they can (Kratochwil 1989). In a hierarchy-as-tyranny system, the provision of collective goods is unproblematic, whereas in an anarchy-as-anomy system (or situation), it is impossible. Alisdair MacIntyre (1998) and Friedrich Kratochwil (1989) have shown that a Hobbesian approach cannot solve the tension between the individually rational and the collectively rational motivations, which should limit the usefulness of any approach based on this metaphor:

> Hobbes makes two incompatible demands of the original contract: he wishes it to be the foundation of all shared and common standards and rules; but he also wishes it to be a contract, and for it to be a contract, there must already exist shared and common standards of the kind which he specifies cannot exist prior to the contract. The concept of an original contract is therefore ruined by internal self-contradiction and cannot be used even to frame a metaphor of a coherent kind. (McIntyre 1998, 137)

Analogously, all efforts to deduce any type of cooperation that is not coincidental co-action in the state of nature is logically impossible. Therefore, cooperation in realism does not deserve the term 'cooperation' but rather 'co-action'. And even if non-cooperative game theory poses to be able to derive norms and information exchange from a state of nature, we are either confronted with a conjuring trick if we believe in the original Hobbesian version of the metaphor, or we have a totally different situation if we assume iteration that actually loses Hobbes' image's barren beauty. What attracts us to the original Hobbesian situation is the sheer impossibility of cooperation and the magic by which Hobbes creates the social contract out of nothing. By introducing iteration, we completely change the imagery, even though we feel that we have merely tweaked the prisoners' dilemma (Axelrod 1984). Now we can still have the shiver of the original state of nature, though without the pain.

However, even if the strong version of this argument as put forth here is not found to be persuasive, one can still argue that certain aspects of interest in international relations cannot be deduced from an iterated state of nature, the most important being communication. Uncooperative game theory cannot derive any meaningful communication from its premises. It denies by assumption its players and actors the ability to imagine the world and being part of collectivities.

By introducing strong external restraints, like the international system or markets, one can even eliminate the difficulties of dealing with decision making by reflective actors, allowing one to exclude situations where by definition we do not have ex ante predictable outcomes. Furthermore, the concepts we use in order to evaluate these outcomes are

96

the causal (elegant and parsimonious) laws of physics, not the messy standards of politics (Weber 1919). Therefore, international relations scholars do not need a theory about politics. This, in turn, is what makes mainstream international relations theory so elegant and parsimonious, so 'natural science-like'.

The popularity of such a view on both the theory and the policy levels has led to a conceptualization of international relations by both scholars and policy makers that excludes politics, persuasion, and rhetoric by assumption. Even complex interdependence theory or mainstream regime theory cannot talk about politics as politics, because they cannot conceptualize language without becoming, in theory, inconsistent (Keohane and Nye 1987). This is surprising, because international relations wants to claim to be part of the tradition of political thinking, although this contradiction is not surprising to anyone who attended an APSA-conference before the Perestroika-movement (Miller 2001).

Mainstream international relations theory is modeled after a quaint Newtonian concept of natural sciences. The political moves to argue this position are the following: International relations follows economics, the discipline international relations scholars respect the most because it is the most natural science-like of the social sciences. Being a natural science is good because it is a positive science and has solved the problem of accumulation, something that we experience every day when we type away at our computers or use an airplane. And since we like our computers, we want a similar paradigm to describe international relations.

This 'folksy' positivism is based on an understanding of science as a cumulative endeavor, based on the metaphor of piling up a mountain and the idea that we can get ever closer to truth, or based on the metaphor of truth as a circle and science as polygons that get ever closer to it.[37] This seems intuitive, and the pressure to legitimize one's discipline in the terms of the natural sciences has been therefore been very strong. One example for this move is the following argument by Nobel Prize winner Paul A. Samuelson in his textbook Economics (1994).

> Economics is not an exact science; yet it is more than an art. We cannot predict with accuracy next year's national income – just as meteorologists cannot forecast next week's weather as precisely as they can tomorrow's. But no bank or big business would be so rash as to consult astrologers rather than trained econometricians, or try to wing it by guess and by gosh. (xxiv)

Even if at first sight, the argument sounds convincing, it is problematic and can be identified as a political argument. Just because there are fields in the natural sciences in which predictions are impossible, such as chaos theory, we cannot deduce that because predictions are also impossible in social sciences, natural and social sciences are therefore analogous. Predictions may be difficult because of com-

---

[37] An extended version of this argument is being made by Friedrich Kratochwil in Evidence, Inference, and Truth as problems of theory building in the social sciences. Munich: unpublished manuscript, 2001.

plexity, but in social sciences they are also difficult because we begin by assuming that our objects of inquiry are actors that can make decisions, imagine their worlds and act upon these imaginations, which necessitates something that Samuelson refers to as the disdained "art."

We will have to accept that if we want to take into account the ability of policy makers to reflect on themselves and their environment and to base actions on these reflections, then we will have problems with them because our actors reflect on our theories about them and amend their behavior if they feel this is necessary, thereby making accumulation impossible by assumption. The qualitative difference between actors and objects should not be ignored only in order to receive the stamp of approval of the scientific community. The dogma of Newtonian natural sciences is expressed very clearly in <u>Designing Social Enquiry</u> by King, Keohane, and Verba (1994, 6). "Precisely defined statistical methods that undergird quantitative research represent abstract formal models applicable to all kinds of research, even that for which variables cannot be measured quantitatively. The very abstract, and even unrealistic, nature of statistical models is what makes the rules of inference shine through so clearly."

Mainstream international relations perceives foundational questions as unproblematic; they are relegated to the scorned discipline of philosophy, while social scientists who want to learn about the facts of the real world only have to follow their method:

> The rules of inference that we discuss are not relevant to all issues that are of significance to social

scientists. Many of the most important questions concerning political life – about such concepts as agency, obligation, legitimacy, citizenship, sovereignty, and the proper relationship between national societies and international politics – are philosophical rather than empirical. But the rules are relevant to all research where the goal is to learn the facts about the real world.(6)

Robert Keohane has made a living of this practice. He has argued since the early 1970s that the conclusions structural realism draws from the core assumption of anarchy are wrong. Thereby he legitimizes the base metaphor of a Hobbesian state of nature (Keohane 1984).

In challenging Waltz, Keohane accepts the role of the Hobbesian metaphor in shaping state behavior. Where Waltz saw conflict, however, Keohane saw the possibility of cooperation. Therefore, the divergence has been over whether cooperation will occur in a world imagined as a Hobbesian state of nature. Under the right conditions, Keohane argues, units can devise strategies of cooperation even in the absence of a strong sovereign to punish defectors (Gourevitch 1999).

By criticizing the conclusions -- not the assumptions -- of Waltzian international relations, Keohane legitimized Waltz' base metaphor. This caused the squabble between Keohane and Waltz to define the legitimate questions in international relations for over a decade (Baldwin 1993). It ended in such scholastic endeavors that were not related to the empirical reality of a post-Cold War world as <u>Neoreal-</u>

ism and Neoliberalism – the Contemporary Debate (1993). These scholars cannot talk about what is interesting in international relations: questions of governance, legitimacy, multilateral conferences, WTO decisions, international law, or human rights, without giving up their core assumptions, which creates *anxiety* not only in the discipline, but in international practice as well. This anxiety will be our starting point to access policy makers in the following chapter.

What Alternatives are there and what Follows From Them?

I have shown that there are problems with the imagery of the international system as a Hobbesian state of nature. However, it is not enough to show that the Hobbesian base metaphor leads to muddled thinking because it only allows certain types of questions. As long as policy makers and scholars subscribe to it, the metaphor will remain relevant. However, in times of transformative change, alternatives arise and compete with the predominant metaphor. Therefore, we need to focus on alternative metaphors that are being offered on the theoretical as well as on the policy levels, regarding the politics of base metaphors that can be described by the metaphorology framework. In order to actually access these politics, give policy makers alternatives, and make them accountable to their principals, we will need therapeutic tools to make policy makers receptive to other metaphors by locally unearthing metaphors in cooperation with them and offering alternative worldviews. How this can be achieved will be the focus of my next chapter.

The question remains as to what metaphor could supersede the Hobbesian imagery. In the debate, two candidates are often mentioned: the network (Zacher 1995) and the language community (Risse 2001). The network, however, is not a free-standing base metaphor, but is linked to the language community metaphor. Think of the lily-in-the-pond imagery that is used to illustrate the power of networks (Kelly 1994). Only if we imagine a frog jumping from lily pad to lily pad, i.e. someone who can benefit from the bridging functionality of the binominally growing lily pads, can we exploit its suggestive power (Negroponte 2002). But even thus amended, the lily-in-the-pond image does not work on its own. The "frogs" using the lily pad network must be able to grasp the potential of the network and understand how it can be used; a frog does not perceive lily pads as a network. Also, the image of the pond blends out network-creation, which necessitates standard-setting which can only be established with the help of language (Shy 2001). This makes it quite clear that the network and language community metaphors are not independent.

The difficulties the lily-in-the-pond image brings with it also explain why network economics so often clash with the basic principles of mainstream economics. When trying to explain how standard-setting--the most important aspect of network-creation -- comes about, we have to admit that political entrepreneurship, which is by definition excluded from economic reckoning, is the only relevant explanatory variable (Shy 2001). A metaphor that allows for communicative action and communication through language is obviously more useful. Thomas Risse introduced communicative action to the American discourse in the popular <u>International Organizations</u> article "Let's Argue" (Risse 2001).

David Ronfeldt and John Arquilla, two senior researchers at the RAND corporation, have worked concepts such as Netwar or *Noopolitik* which integrate the network image with the language community metaphor (Arquilla, Ronfeldt 1996; 1997; 1999; 2001). Noopolitik is based on the idea of a knowledge sphere, a broader form of cyberspace, and offers an alternative framework to view international relations. Interesting about this specific project is its nexus to the policy level. The project was in fact sponsored by the Office of the Assistant Secretary of Defense/Command, Control, Communications, and Intelligence (OASD/C3I), and was conducted within both the Acquisition and Technology Policy Center and the International Security and Defense Policy Center of RAND's National Defense Research Institute (NDRI), and was directed at policy makers in the hope of changing their conception of the international realm (Arquilla, Ronfeldt 1999). Therefore, it can be situated on the policy level.[38] They argue,

> in our view, a new paradigm is needed—in fact, it is already emerging—which we call noopolitik (nü-oh-poh-li-teek). This is the form of statecraft that we argue will come to be associated with the noosphere, the broadest informational realm of the mind (from the Greek noos) under which cyberspace (i.e., the Net) and the infosphere (cyberspace plus the media) are subsumed. Noopolitik is foreign-policy behavior for the information age that emphasizes the primacy of ideas, values, norms, laws, and ethics—it would work through "soft power" rather than "hard power." Noopolitik is guided more by a conviction that right makes for might, than

---

[38] The success was mixed. The researchers got increased funding, however, government interest in the concept was minimal (personal communication with David Ronfeldt).

by the obverse. Both state and nonstate actors may be guided by noopolitik; but rather than being state-centric, its strength may likely stem from enabling state and nonstate actors to work con-jointly. The driving motivation of noopolitik cannot be national interests defined in statist terms. National interests will still play a role, but they may be defined more in societywide than state-centric terms and be fused with broader, even global, interests in enhancing the transnationally networked "fabric" in which the players are embedded. While realpolitik tends to empower states, noopolitik will likely empower networks of state and nonstate actors. Realpolitik pits one state against another, but noopolitik encourages states to cooperate in coalitions and other mutual frameworks.

If we consider the shared characteristics of many post-Hobbesian approaches to international relations, we notice their focus on the language community metaphor. The base metaphor of language shared by actors, thus forming a community, is intuitively very powerful. Aristotle introduced this base metaphor in the first book of Politics (Aristotle 1984) in his distinction between humans and animals:

> Now, that man is more of a political animal than bees or any other gregarious animals is evident. Nature, as we often say, makes nothing in vain, and man is the only animal whom she has endowed with the gift of speech. And whereas mere voice is but an indication of pleasure or pain, and is therefore found in other animals (for their nature attains to the per-

ception of pleasure and pain and the intimation of them to one another, and no further), the power of speech is intended to set forth the expedient and inexpedient, and therefore likewise the just and the unjust. And it is a characteristic of man that he alone has any sense of good and evil, of just and unjust, and the like, and the association of living beings who have this sense makes a family and a state.

Aristotle then juxtaposes the metaphor with an image that is logically equivalent to the Hobbesian state of nature that forms the base metaphor for mainstream international relations. "And he who by nature and not by mere accident is without a state, is either a bad man or above humanity; he is like the "tribeless, lawless, hearthless one, whom Homer denounces, the natural outcast is forthwith a lover of war; he may be compared to an isolated piece at draughts" (Aristotle 1984, book I 1253a).

The question, then, is why the language community metaphor seems such an attractive candidate to supersede international Hobbesianism. Functionally, the language community metaphor can better conceptualize the practice of the international realm, because it can describe reflexivity and the imagination of collectivity. Policy makers seem to like this metaphor because it seems consistent with their practice. But from what does it derive persuasive power? Why is it coming into fashion now? How does it relate to globalization?

This, of course, is a political question; therefore, by definition, no final, causal answer can be given, though a

106

historical perspective might unearth its development (Blumenberg 1998).

One can argue that the most important trend in philosophy of the 20th century was the *linguistic turn*, the newly-won conviction that language is not the medium transporting thought, but that thought cannot exist outside of language (Rorty 1967). From this basic assumption follows that are no facts outside language, and no reality other than that which presents itself under some linguistic description. Philosophy about language is as old as philosophy itself; however, the realization that no thinking can take place outside of language is relatively new. It was first introduced in the late 19th and early 20th centuries by Gottlob Frege and Bertrand Russell, and then expanded into various directions by Ludwig Wittgenstein and others (Rorty 1967).

This change of perspective in philosophy has reverberated through many disciplines in the natural and social sciences, as well as in the humanities. Although it seems interesting for philosophy, why should it matter for international relations? The discipline of international relations had not been influenced by the linguistic turn until recently. Theorists emulated a Newtonian understanding of natural sciences even in the 1990s, with the goal of finally uncovering the laws of nature. Gary King, Robert Keohane and Sidney Verba (1994) argue that facts "can be collected by qualitative or quantitative researchers more or less systematically, and the former is obviously better than the latter..." Furthermore, because Cold War-era policy makers traditionally stuck to rather simple constructs of the international realm, their actions corresponded neatly to the theory (Lebow 1998).

However, the recent linguistic turn is gradually impacting international relations on different levels. It questions the subject-object distinction, challenges the ahistorical epistemology of structural realism by arguing that social truth is practice-specific, and has formed the philosophical grounding for a more sophisticated understanding of norms as more than intervening variables (Kratochwil 1989). These are all very useful and important crosspollinations, though the most important aspect of the culture of the linguistic turn is that for the first time since the debate on the League of Nations (Wilson, 1919) it makes the base metaphor of the international realm as a language community attractive.

The Politics of Base Metaphors

A decision for one of the several metaphors is inherently political. It structures expectations on the policy level and it predetermines the types of questions that can be asked on the theory level.

The culture of the Enlightenment has biased scholars towards a conceptualization of the international realm as an anarchic state of nature, because it can be more easily operationalized in natural science terms, i.e. more geometrico (Hobbes 1998) and it supposedly works without hermeneutically understanding the beliefs of its objects of analysis. R. B. J Walker argues (1993),

For early-modern writers like Hobbes, reason and order – both cosmological and socio-political – could be envisaged in relation to the discovery of permanent principles, the secular guarantees of a geometry that seemed to offer at least as good a bet as the increasingly dubious guarantees of Heaven.

However, by excluding cooperation and community in the international realm, we dismiss communication as a meaningful phenomenon. In an acommunal realm, only 'voice,' in Aristotelian terms, or signaling, as Thomas Schelling refers to it, are possible (1967). This leads to a noncooperative game theory and to such scholastic endeavors as trying to square the circle and explain cooperation in a multi-person prisoners' dilemma (Axelrod 1984; 1997). This is done by introducing auxiliary assumptions that supposedly are in congruence with the prisoners' dilemma, i.e. iteration or ad hoc auxiliary assumptions like the exclusion of backward induction on psychological grounds, as has been done by Robert Axelrod (1984). This is supported through social experiments, in which students as 'rational actors' succeed by employing tit-for-tat strategies. This conjuring trick is then applied analogously to explain cooperation in the international realm.

However, as has been shown before, Hobbesianism cannot resolve the tension between individual rational and collectively rational; it does not allow a trajectory from the state of nature to cooperation (Kratochwil 1989). Therefore, all efforts to deduce any type of cooperation that is more than coincidental co-action from the state of nature is logically impossible. If, however, we want to describe, explain, or predict cooperation, we need a theory that can do that.

The language community metaphor, on the other hand, has no problem explaining communication <u>and</u> the breakdown of communication. Just as the term 'to lie' can only be used sensibly if a common assumption of trustworthiness exists, cooperation can explain the breakdown of cooperation (Kratochwil 1989). Therefore, the speech metaphor seems to be the more powerful 'operating system' to run international relations on.

However, we cannot directly access which metaphor is true. Following Blumenberg, the truth of metaphors is pragmatic; therefore, we can only ask what type of political arguments are being made for a base metaphor of the language community or the base metaphor of an anarchic state of nature. On what side are policy makers leaning in this political game?

A language community does not imply a world state in the idealist sense. It merely gives us the tools to describe the success and breakdown of cooperation between individuals and collectives by utilizing a vocabulary that is adequate for the social sciences. We can focus on issues such as public diplomacy without seeming absolutely silly or cynical, because we can actually assign relevance to language and how it influences how policy makers -- be they politicians or foreign publics -- imagine the international realm or a specific bilateral relation.

Conclusion

This chapter has shown that the current crisis in the discipline of international relations can best be described by utilizing the meta-vocabulary of base metaphors, thereby unearthing the politics of base metaphors. In order to deal with the particular nature of the discipline of international relations as a social science, a focus on both the theory and policy levels is important.

The theoretical parsimony of the anarchy paradigm and its ability to explain social behavior with natural science methodology have made it successful on both the theory and policy levels. However, empirical developments, the linguistic turn, the interest in communication networks, and increasing international political interdependence have shown the weaknesses of this approach. Although it can conceptualize signaling, it is not able to conceptualize meaningful communication.

With the linguistic turn and globalization, the metaphor of language communities has gained popularity and a community that allows political discourse about legitimacy, and justice in an international realm is becoming the working metaphor of policy makers and some theorists. Describing this process as a political process where different base metaphors lead to different potential scenarios delegitimizes any paradigm that takes its legitimization from natural correspondence with reality, and therefore opens up space for alternative conceptualizations. This means that perhaps we are at a phase in the discourse in international relations where paradigmatic change might happen and where Copernicus can persuade Mother Earth to give up her center spot. This process of uncovering and recovering the political realm must be a therapeutic process, which will be the focus of the next chapter.

Imag[in]ing Globalization: Therapy for Policy Makers

In chapter four, I introduce a technique that allows us to reveal the political dimension of base metaphors by engaging the policy maker in a therapeutic relationship. I will use the example of how policy makers perceive globalization, because that example also enables us to understand the political opportunities of global transformative change. The technique I propose is called *philosophical therapy*, a four step procedure based on the work of Ludwig Wittgenstein.

The point is not to show that metaphysical uses of words are grammatical mistakes, but rather to persuade an interlocutor that he has no good reasons for making them, that he can simply drop them and thereby eliminate certain disquiets or dissatisfaction. Getting rid of metaphysical questions is voluntary, an exercise of an individual's freedom.

(Gordon Baker 2000)

Globalization and Transformative Change: Revisiting the Second Problem of Chapter 1

In the last chapter, I presented a framework (metaphorology) that allows us to describe the politics of transformative change by focusing on the base metaphors that structure our worlds. In this chapter, I propose a technique that allows us to access the politics of base metaphors by therapeutically engaging the policy maker. This will allow us to give options to the policy makers to envision the world differently and to empower their principals to question the policy makers' world views. As an example, I propose a reflection on the term *globalization*, enabling us to better understand the transformative change that is taking place.

Globalization depoliticizes by restraining the decisions of political actors (Strange 1994). Therefore, the task for the politically-minded is clear: It is our responsibility to regain political territory and open up political spaces--to uncover and recover the political realm. This can be done by pointing at contexts that in the traditional narrative are considered neutral, unproblematic, or determined, but that hide political decisions. By doing so, we offer options to policy makers and assign accountability for decisions. This simple thought drives the following inquiry.

Addressing the understanding of policy makers matters in the globalization debate, because globalization is an emergent phenomenon, shaped by and shaping our imagination of the world. On the policy level the world is imagined and policy makers act accordingly. The metaphorological approach allows us to describe this level. By nurturing the understanding of policy makers for this level we increase their accountability. The approach I propose is (a) grammatical, i.e. it asks the question, "How do we use the concept?" and (b) therapeutic, i.e. it offers a local clarification of the use of words achieved through cooperative deliberation with an interlocutor. These interlocutors are policy makers.

My approach is based on Wittgenstein's philosophical therapy. It is an approach that makes visible the images underlying our use of concepts, showing in what ways they are problematic, and offering alternative images. I will describe it as a four-step procedure that has the goal of reducing anxiety about globalization, increasing policy makers' freedom to make decisions, and empowering their principals. By increasing their freedom, we force them to take responsibility for their policies. In the following section, I will outline the procedure and then apply it by focusing on our usage of the term *globalization* from four perspectives.

The Procedure of Philosophical Therapy

During World War II, Professors Robert Grant and Basil Reeve of the University of Newcastle were writing a book on wound shock and found that the symptoms they were observing in their patients with wound shock were very dissimilar (Grant, Reeve 1944). Ludwig Wittgenstein worked as an assistant nurse for the professors. He suggested that in order to make clear that the term *wound shock* applied to a syndrome used to describe disparate symptoms and was not a naturally given category, but rather one established conventionally, the term should be printed upside down to constantly remind the reader of its problematic nature. In the end, however, the publisher decided against this idea because it would have been too costly. Even in this age of computers it has not become cheaper to play this type of game. Therefore, try to imagine 'globalization' written upside-down!

In the following paragraphs, I sketch the approach that aims to clarify the usage of language and to dissolve some of the discomforts we have with the term *globalization*. The goal of the therapeutic procedure is not to ultimately define or redefine globalization, but to dissolve discomforts we have about the concept and thereby increase the freedom of decision makers. This dissolution consists of making the meaning of the words used in putting the question so clear to ourselves that we are released from the spell the term casts on us (Waismann 1968, 10) Friedrich Waismann argues in How I see Philosophy (1968) that in philosophy, the real problem is not to find the answer to a given question, but to find a sense for it (7). He continues, "We are trying to catch the shadows cast by the opacities of speech. A wrong analogy absorbed into the forms of our language produces mental discomfort (and the feeling of discomfort, when it refers to language, is a profound one)."

The procedure I am proposing is called *philosophical therapy*. It offers a family of methods, clarification, dissolution, and the shifting of metaphors to deal with philosophical problems.[39] It is not a language-cleaning algorithm, to clear language of misuses once and for all, but an individualized therapy with the goal of the <u>local</u> clarification of the usage of language and the construction of alternative plausible images, in order to increase the freedom of the thinker. By increasing the freedom of the thinker, we recapture moments of decision, i.e. moments of politics where policy makers can change the course of events and we as constituents can hold them accountable.

---

[39] The family concept is based on Wittgensteins picture of familiarities as interlocking fibers forming a rope. Philosophical Investigations, article 67.

Philosophical therapy has some interesting features. The interlocutor is not forced to comply; he is left free to select, accept or reject any way of using his words. The only thing that one has to insist upon is that the interlocutor use words consciously. The aim is not to confirm or invalidate any ahistorical truth. Philosophical therapy aims to describe, not to explain. Friedrich Waismann argues (12),

> an explanation, in the sense of a deductive proof, cannot satisfy us because it pushes the question, 'Why just these rules and no other ones?"' only one stage back. In following that method, we do not *want* to give reasons. All we do is to describe a use or tabulate rules. In doing this, we are not making any discoveries: there is nothing to be discovered in grammar. Grammar is autonomous and not dictated by reality. Giving reasons, bound as it is to come to an end and leading to something which cannot further be explained, *ought* not to satisfy us. In grammar we never ask the question 'why?'

The tactic in the procedure of philosophical therapy is (a) to bring a challenge to a dogma, (b) to expose a picture that stands behind this dogma, (c) to propose an alternative picture of concept-application, and (d) to deflect anxieties about this new model (Baker 2000, 32). This is a personalized endeavor, similar to a psychoanalytical therapy.[40]

---

[40]For the Freudian approach see (Freud 1991). Psycho-analytical therapy aims for empathetic understanding of the interlocutor, while philosophical therapy poses stronger consistency requirements.

This understanding of philosophical therapy is not shared by all Wittgenstein scholars. Hacker (1999) would argue that philosophical therapy aims to solve philosophical problems "once and for all." Philosophical therapy seen from this perspective aims to expose the misuses of words (i.e. mistakes in grammar) by simply confronting the discourse with descriptions of how words are correctly used (i.e. linguistic facts). This perspective can be based on paragraph II, sentence 1, § 133 of the <u>Philosophical Investigation</u>: "For the clarity that we are aiming at is indeed *complete* clarity". [41] An example of this way of seeing Wittgenstein's philosophy is Gordon P. Baker and Peter M.S. Hacker's <u>Wittgenstein: Rules, Grammar and Necessity</u> (1985, 25.2-3):

> Philosophy... is a grammatical investigation (§90) on which philosophical problems are resolved and misunderstanding eliminated by describing our use of words, clarifying *the grammar* of expressions and tabulating rules (WWK 184). .... If someone ... claims that colours are sensations in the mind or in the brain, the philosopher must point out that this person is *misusing* the words 'sensation' and 'colour'. Sensations in the brain, he should remind his interlocutor, are called 'headaches,' and colours are not headaches; one can have (i. e. it makes sense to speak of) sensations in the knee or in the back, but not in the mind. It is, he must stress, extended things that are coloured. ... It is a grammatical observation, viz.

---

[41] Article 133, Philosophical Investigations.

that the grammar of colour licenses predicating 'is coloured' (primarily) of things of which one may also predicate 'is extended.' And minds and sensations are not extended, i. e. it *makes no sense to say* 'This pain is 5cm long' ... [In this way we correct] the wayward interlocutor ... [Emphasis added]

Wittgenstein has been well known for the dissolution and conceptual shifting of philosophical problems: e.g. rule following as a practice (Wittgenstein 1958, § 202), thinking as 'the activity of operating with signs.' He has been less known for the method of philosophical therapy that he demonstrates with these examples. A closer reading of § 133 makes it clear that it is not the resolution of problems once and for all that interests him, "For the clarity that we are aiming at is indeed *complete* clarity. But this simply means that the philosophical problems should *completely* disappear." He continues:

The real discovery is the one that makes me capable of stopping doing philosophy when I want to. -- The one that gives philosophy peace, so that it is no longer tormented by questions which bring in question. -- Instead, we now demonstrate a method, by examples; and the series of examples can be broken off. -- Problems are solved (difficulties eliminated), not a single problem.

There is not a philosophical method, though there are indeed methods, like different therapies.[42]

It even suggests that he does not offer philosophical therapy as an algorithmic procedure to solve these problems, but only offers an idea that can be the basis of a number of methods. Gordon Baker describes this with the picture of an argument with an interlocutor who has to be persuaded (27):

> The crucial move must be to persuade an individual interlocutor to renounce the prejudice expressed by statements featuring the words 'must' and 'cannot,' or better, persuading another to rid his thinking of these deeply entrenched notions (Denkgewohnheiten) and of deep desires to see things in certain ways The therapy focuses on bringing to another's consciousness neglected possibilities; on winning sincere acknowledgement of possibilities which he had previously excluded. Nothing else can liberate an individual from various forms of prejudice or change his way of looking at things.

One example in which Wittgenstein applies philosophical therapy is his dissolution of our understanding of categories as boxes into which we put things that have common characteristics, by asking what is it that lets us distinguish what games are. Therefore, by categorizing his method into a four step procedure, we lose some of the flexibility that

---

[42] Article 133, Philosophical Investigations.

Wittgenstein introduces into philosophy, but gain a better understanding of the approach.[43] It should be seen more as an example that describes a way of thinking, rather than an ideal type of a procedure that is to be applied. We have to keep that in mind when we argue that the procedure requires four steps. These steps can be referred to as the following: (a) to bring a challenge to a dogma, (b) to expose a picture that stands behind this dogma, (c) to propose an alternative picture of concept-application, and (d) to deflect anxieties about this new model. In order to develop an understanding for this procedure, I will follow the text. Wittgenstein challenges the dogma by arguing (1958, § 66):

> Consider for example the proceedings that we call "games". I mean board-games, card-games, ball-games, Olympic games, and so on. What is common to them all? -- Don't say: "There must be something common, or they would not be called 'games' "-but look and see whether there is anything common to all.

He exposes our picture of categorizing things by challenging, "There must be something common, or they would not be called 'games'" and clarifies the problem.

> For if you look at them you will not see something that is common to all, but similarities, relationships, and a whole series of them at that. To repeat: don't think, but look!

---

[43] In the following chapters I will apply the framework less stringently.

Look for example at board-games, with their multifarious relationships.

Now pass to card-games; here you find many correspondences with the first group, but many common features drop out, and others appear.

When we pass next to ball-games, much that is common is retained, but much is lost.-- Are they all 'amusing'? Compare chess with noughts and crosses. Or is there always winning and losing, or competition between players? Think of patience. In ball games there is winning and losing; but when a child throws his ball at the wall and catches it again, this feature has disappeared. Look at the parts played by skill and luck; and at the difference between skill in chess and skill in tennis.

Think now of games like ring-a-ring-a-roses; here is the element of amusement, but how many other characteristic features have disappeared! sometimes similarities of detail.
And we can go through the many, many other groups of games in the same way; can see how similarities crop up and disappear.

In the next step of the procedure he proposes an alternative picture of how we conceptualize games.

And the result of this examination is: we see a complicated network of similarities overlapping and cries-crossing: sometimes overall similarities.

I can think of no better expression to characterize these similarities than "family resemblances;" for the various resemblances between members of a family: build, features, colour of eyes, gait, temperament, etc. etc. overlap and cries-cross in the same way.-And I shall say: 'games' form a family.

And in the fourth step, he deflects our anxiety about this new way of seeing games by arguing:

"But if the concept 'game' is uncircumscribed like that, you don't really know what you mean by a 'game.'" -- When I give the description: "The ground was quite covered with plants" --do you want to say I don't know what I am talking about until I can give a definition of a plant? My meaning would be explained by, say, a drawing and the words "The ground looked roughly like this." Perhaps I even say "it looked exactly like this."-Then were just this grass and these leaves there, arranged just like this? No, that is not what it means. And I should not accept any picture as exact in this sense.

By walking us through the process of challenging a dogma, exposing a picture that stands behind this dogma, proposing an alternative picture of concept-application, and deflecting anxieties about this new model, policy makers are led through a procedure in which they learn to give up long-held misunderstandings that have caused us anxiety. It is a highly personalized philosophy, but it exposes room for political decisions that has become scarce in times of transformative change. Someone who never felt that by categorizing all members of a group, these members need to share at least one characteristic, will not find the argument persuasive or even interesting. Philosophical therapy is a personalized endeavor, similar to a psychoanalytical therapy.

This means the types of questions about globalization that such an approach can ask are different. They allow us to talk to policy makers on the level where the world is imagined. The thrust of my argument will not be to offer a new definition of globalization, but to put some of the policy makers' discomforts to rest and to increase their freedom. Increasing their freedom reintroduces politics and a discourse about accountability and responsibility.

I will do this by observing globalization in its natural habitat, language. One might question my choice of language if goods are being traded, investments made, and actual human beings are beings are transported by such people-movers as airplanes and trains. However, if we look at the distinctness of the things that are being exchanged and the ideas we subsume under the concept globalization, it becomes clear that it is a linguistic category--not a natural kind.

Different scholars, policy makers, and publics conceptualize globalization in different ways (Cox 1997; Keck, Sikkink 1998). However, the mainstream discourse shares one common feature: conceptualizing globalization by reifying it into a causal variable (Sassen 1996; Barber 1995; Bauman 1998; Friedman 1999).

This can be an independent variable (globalization leading to integration and disintegration) or dependent variable (technological and cultural change leading to globalization), but this differentiation between globalization as an independent or dependent variable is often sloppily formulated.[44] I will arguethat the reification of globalization into a variable has to do with the images we use to understand the concept. These images normally reside the background (Fauconnier 1997). Dealing with these mental images is an important aspect of thinking about globalization, because our beliefs about globalization themselves are what shape globalization.

Surfing the Wave: Globalization as a Causal Force

People see globalization as threatening. Beneath the understanding of globalization as a reified variable lurks the im-

---

[44] This argument applies to the main stream and our common usage of the term globalization. See for example, Anthony Giddens' Runaway World: how globalisation is reshaping our lives (1999).

age of a natural force, or more concretely, a wave.[45] The following examples by policy makers show how internalized the reified variable metaphor of globalization as a natural force is in the policy-making discourse:

As globalization sweeps the world, many areas, Africa especially, wonder if this tidal wave is good or bad for them.[46]

Faced with popular demands for greater self-determination, national governments around the world are under pressure to devolve power to the local level. In this context, globalization is like a giant wave that can either capsize nations or carry them forward on its crest.[47]

Like a great natural force, globalization offers major opportunities for and perils to the possibilities for human flourishing. Characterized by the rapid spread of market systems, the extraordinary advances in science and technology, continuing urbanization, and changing demographics, Globaliza-

---

[45] E. g. Nicholas D. Kristof "Experts Question Roving Flow of Global Capital." New York Times, September 20, 1998. Tagliabue, John. "International Merger Wave Catches Europe's Law Firms." New York Times, August 4, 2000, Cohen, Roger. "The Cries of Welfare States Under the Knife." New York Times, September 19, 1997.

[46] Adam Dieng, assistant secretary-general of the United Nations, in The International Herald Tribune, August 21st, 2001, 6.

[47] Shahid Yusuf, senior economic adviser at the World Bank, International Herald Tribune, September 17, 1999.

tion can become a positive unifying bond for humanity; or it can pose a major threat to human relations, cultural traditions, and a sense of personal identity.[48]

A tide of economic liberalization has swept across the world over the past two decades. It is creating vast opportunities. But the question arises whether today's integrating world economy will be more durable than that of a century ago.[49]

These and other comments expose globalization's base image and the dissatisfaction with the globalization debate. This seems to be where the 'philosophical problem' of globalization is located.

By showing that the image underlying mainstream globalization discourse is problematic and by offering alternative images, the globalization discourse can be re-politicized. Perhaps new policy options will emerge.

The dogma challenged in this example is the common conception of globalization. Can we really understand the phenomenon by asking what is caused by globalization, or, consequently, what is causing globalization? This seems doubtful.

---

[48] "Globalization and the Human Condition. An Introduction." <u>Aspen Institute 50th Anniversary Symposium</u>, August 19–22, Aspen, CO.
[49] Martin Wolf, "The Dangers of Protectionism.", <u>Financial Times</u>, November 8, 2000, 21.

In the next step, one has to persuade the interlocutor of the problematic nature of the concept by exposing a picture that informs this dogma. The dogma of seeing globalization as a reified variable is based on globalization as a natural force, a tidal wave sweeping across the world destroying welfare states and introducing sport utility vehicles to the world (Giddens 1999). Even though this description is an exaggeration, the image of globalization as a natural force is constantly with us. Whenever we argue about globalization and are not careful, this conceptualization of globalization as a natural force can very easily happen even to the best of us. We sometimes will rely on the imagery of the wave when picturing globalization. Or, as Gordon Baker argues, the act of "Bringing to consciousness this whole set of interlinked pictures belongs to the therapeutic activity of exploring the motives for falling into philosophical confusion." (2000, 33).

In a third step, we need to propose an alternative picture of concept-application. In the case of globalization this can be the picture of a discourse. Globalization does not take place outside of language. If there were no word for it, we would not cluster together such distinct phenomena as the global spread of Microsoft WindowsXP, nationalism, and Britney Spears. Globalization is a concept that is utilized to make claims, both claims about the truth and politics. By making these claims, we aim to persuade, to argue, to threaten, and to charm. Imagining globalization as a discourse of heterogeneous groups that are making political arguments can replace the image of globalization as a natural force.

But can we deflect the anxieties about this new model? What does such a discourse do? How can it help us understand globalization? How does it influence the real world? Has our therapy been successful? No, it cannot be this easy. If we ask these questions, we show that we have not yet left the imagery of cause and effect. It shows how deeply ingrained is this conception of globalization as something that does something to us. Understanding globalization as a discourse should lead to questions like: Who is accountable? Why is group A making this argument? What is the legitimating claim of this argument? If we smuggle the reified variable back into the discourse by analyzing a 'discourse about a reified variable,' we fall back into our old position. Therefore, we need to look closely at the specific aspects of the discourse metaphor where the usage of globalization is problematic. To assure that our therapy is successful and that our policy makers do not fall back into the old state of imag[in]ing globalization as a wave, we need to tackle the subject from more than one angle.

Duck-Rabbit

We use the term *globalization* in active form and in passive form. The dictionary definition exemplifies this ambiguity (Webster's 1993): "Globalization: the act of globalizing or condition of being globalized." Globalization read in active form is an independent variable; while read in passive form it becomes a dependent variable. Our understanding and usage of the concept have important repercussions on how we see the politics of globalization. We can switch between the two perspectives, or aspects of a phenomena, though we have a preference for one or the other. Wittgenstein describes this vexing moment of aspect-seeing in <u>The Philosophical Investigation</u>.[50] "I shall call the following figure, derived from Jastrow[1], the duck-rabbit. It can be seen as a rabbit's head or as a duck's."

He continues, "And I must distinguish between the 'continuous seeing' of an aspect and the 'dawning' of an aspect. The picture might have been shown to me, and I never have seen anything but a rabbit in it" (Wittgenstein 1969, 1994). Policy makers perceive the concept of globalization as an event, taking place, impacting lives (in the active

---

[50] "A visually ambiguous drawing, introduced by J. Jastrow. It can be perceived either as a duck or as a rabbit, but not both simultaneously. It constitutes the starting-point for Wittgenstein's study, in Philosophical Investigations, ii. ix, of aspect perception. It exemplifies the concept-laden character of some forms of perception, and provides a connecting link to examination of the perception of speech and writing." in: <u>Oxford Companion to Philosophy</u> (1995).

form), or as a result of a development (in the passive form). A protester at the World Economic Forum in Davos will see the conference differently than a participating politician. One can, by concentrating, or by pure coincidence, see the other aspect. However, one must distinguish between the aspect one sees steadily and the aspect that suddenly flashes up.

This changing quality of the concept of globalization is not caused by deficient thinking, but rather is a situation where the grammar of the concept is indeterminate. By accepting this indeterminacy, we become aware of the fact that some questions concerning globalization cannot be answered sensibly at all levels of abstraction.

Glocaligration: Global + Local, Integration + Fragmentation

James Rosenau introduced the concept of *fragmegration*, a combination of integration and fragmentation, into the globalization discourse (Rosenau 1997). "We are in a new epoch. It is an epoch that is based on contradictions, on uncertainties, on what I call 'fragmegration.' That's a combination of fragmentation and integration".[51] *Glocalization*, i.e. globalization + localization, became the en vogue explana-

---

[51] Interview with James N. Rosenau. August 4, 1997. The interview can be found at: http://www.csis.org/ics/dia/introsen.html.

tion for the dynamic of globalization (Ohmae 1995). This practice of coining words enables us to express globalization as a paradoxical phenomenon (Naisbitt 1994).

By accepting contradiction in terms of a component of globalization, we feel that we describe a concept that defies our normal linear logic. The image of an Escher-esque world appalls and attracts us. In the paradoxical nature of globalization its power is manifested. What type of phenomenon is this that can actually transcend normal logic?

However, to a large extent what we perceive as paradox is just muddled thinking. When we argue that globalization leads to homogenization and disintegration, at the same time we compound two different phenomena that are taking place on different conceptual levels. Or as James Rosenau argues, "A way to understand the world today is to understand that not only are there forces at work that are in the direction of fragmentation, localization, decentralization on the one-hand, and forces at work towards globalization, centralization, and integration on the other hand, but most importantly these are interactive and casually related."[52] A reconstruction of the argument, therefore, dissolves the paradox.

It's almost the case that every increment of integration gives rise to an increment of fragmentation and vice-versa. The way to understand the world: it's not chaos, but it is complexity; it's a world of endless feedback. It's a mistake to think in narrow time frames in terms of cause and effect within a particular time frame because

---

[52] Interview with James N. Rosenau (1997).

every effect becomes a cause in the next stage of time. What fragmegration does or involves is the close inter-action between distant events and very local events. [53]

The *module nationalism* spreads globally and when imple-mented, leads to disintegrative acts by political actors. By breaking the argument down into two steps, the dissemina-tion of the module nationalism and the effect of the module nationalism, we dissolve the paradox.

The same can be done for glocalization. Globalization, again defined as a driver, leads to the dissemination of products, information, and ideas. On the local level, these are accepted. However, after a threshold level is reached, local products, information, and ideas are perceived as more valuable. Therefore, in order to increase dissemina-tion of global products, they must be localized. The argu-ment here is not very sophisticated; however it is interest-ing that by reconstructing the glocaligration paradoxes step-by-step, they lose their paradoxical attractiveness.

Selection Bias

Policy makers often have a Darwinesque understanding of globalization. They feel that globalization selects the fittest organizations and destroys the rest (Sahtouris 1997). This evolutionary image of globalization evokes a vocabulary of

---

[53] Interview with James N. Rosenau (1997).

selection, adaptation, regulatory races to the bottom, the competition state, etc.

Evolution is very well entrenched in mainstream thinking, and by relying on this image, policy makers forget that it is only a metaphor, and that the logic of social life functions differently. Anthony Giddens argues in The Constitution of Society that "[b]iology has been taken to provide a guide to conceptualizing the structure and the functioning of social systems and to analyzing processes of evolution via mechanisms of adaptation" (Giddens 1984, 1).

In the chapter "Change, Evolution, and Power," he deconstructs the usage of biological metaphors in social theories (229-263). The logic of evolutionary biology posits that unconscious random changes in the DNA of living beings lead to differentiations, which are then selected by the environment. If one of the random changes fits the environment well, then this living organism can potentially reproduce more often (Maturana, Varela 1992).

In social life, we assume that actors have the ability to reflect on and decide on strategies. These are moments of freedom in which they can choose. However, when we see growing homogeneity in the international system, such as similar economic, social, and environmental policies in developing and developed countries, we intuitively feel that selection is at work. However, it does not have to be explained by the imagery of evolution, but may be better described by the alternative image of children in the schoolyard who emulate their 'leader of the pack.' Governments emulate policies in order to legitimize their position in the international community. This means that processes we imagine as natural selection can often be better described as emulation processes (Meyer 1997).

By proposing an alternative image, we can offer alternative strategic options to policy makers. When imagining globalization as an evolutionary selection process, the responsible policy maker has to adapt, whereas if globalization is imagined as an emulation process, a responsible policy maker can reflect consciously on her decisions. The inevitability of globalization loses its power and we increase the freedom of choice for the policy makers.

Conclusion

Globalization is a social phenomenon and theories about globalization flow directly into the policy making process. In times of transformative change our imagination of the world becomes a political question. This recursive relationship between theory and policy makes it important to address the policy makers. As long as policy makers understand globalization through the imagery of a wave, it will create restraints on state capacity. They will aim to adapt to globalization.

By challenging the mainstream understanding, unearthing the politics of globalization, offering an alternative images of globalization, and addressing the individual policy maker locally, the grammatical and therapeutic approach enables us to help policy makers ask new questions and develop different policies. Approaching the imagery underlying globalization from four different sides (Wave, Duck-Rabbit, Escher, and Evolution) emphasizes the deeply-rooted conceptions of globalization. The very individual and local project of the grammatical and therapeutic approach is of general importance, insofar as it offers a way to access policy makers, increase their freedom, and make them accountable to their principals. By ascribing freedom to policy makers, we change the discourse from one of necessity to one of politics and ethics. After having introduced the procedure of philosophical therapy, let us focus on public diplomacy.

The Politics of Communicating Foreign Policy

In chapter five, I focus on the policy level debate on communicating foreign policy in a globalizing world, applying the type of perspective developed in the preceding chapters. I analyze the public diplomacy discourse in the aftermath of the September 11, 2001, terrorist attacks, focusing on the metaphors and general concepts policy makers use to explain their investment in public diplomacy.

138

Attention Taliban! You are condemned. Did you know
that?[54]

The Politics of Public Diplomacy

This chapter asks what role the policy level ascribes to the communication of foreign policy in the aftermath of September 11, applying the type of critical thinking developed in the preceding chapters. It will show the relevance of asking these types of questions in times of transformative change. We will be able to observe how the base understandings of the international realm are contested and debates about how we imagine the world have become part of standard political practice. A special focus on U.S. foreign policy is warranted due to its influence on the constitutive norms of the international realm.

If we use the discourse on public diplomacy to judge the U.S. foreign policy makers' understanding of the international system, we will find that policy makers have moved beyond a realpolitik approach. However, we will also find that there is not one main metaphor explaining public diplomacy. Most policy makers rely on metaphors

---

[54] Official Pentagon broadcast from an EC-130 radio plane to the Taliban in Afghanistan.

from the domestic realm, such as branding or spin control, and acknowledge the relevance of the issue, though no generally accepted framework has developed. A tension exists between conceptualizations that aim at strategic influence and conceptualizations that aim for communicative dialogue.

The oft-voiced truism that everything has changed after September 11 carries critical potential. If indeed everything has changed, we need to re-evaluate our base assumptions about everything. This means that in addition to imagining a globalizing world, we need to deal with a post 9-11 world. This chapter will deal with a very specific aspect of this everything, namely the field of public diplomacy with a metaphorological framework that enables us to describe how policy makers frame the subject (chapter 3).

Realpolitik-oriented policy makers ridicule the idea that communication-- instead of force--should play an important role in American foreign policy, preferring the inherently violent metaphor of a "war against terrorism" (Miller 2002; Walt 2002). Others claim that winning the hearts and minds of the Arab population is crucial to avoiding future violent conflict. Therefore, with the stakes higher than ever before, the debate on the role of public diplomacy has developed new urgency. The subject of public diplomacy is relevant and conceptual confusion on this issue in the aftermath of September 11 warrants a closer look at the politics of base metaphors in public diplomacy.

Public diplomacy is a vital, yet understudied field (chapter 2). As stated in chapter 1, public diplomacy is a government activity designed to generate foreign support for U.S. policies. However, it can tell us a lot about foreign policy in general. I will argue that policy makers' selection of metaphors to describe public diplomacy determines to a large extent the practice of foreign policy and the field of public diplomacy. Therefore, if we are interested in unearthing the political dimensions of how we conceptualize public diplomacy, we need to focus on the policy level where the international realm is imagined and then acted upon, which we can do by applying the metaphorology framework introduced in chapter 3. A therapeutic approach that focuses on the imagery underlying public diplomacy is needed to access the policy makers, enabling them and empowering their principals. This, in turn, can help us understand more generally the politics of foreign policy in times of transformative change.

The metaphors policy makers use to frame the abstract practice of public diplomacy are not theoretically innocent and not independent of the broader conception they have of the international realm. Therefore, in order to access the politics of public diplomacy, one could argue that we primarily need to look at the metaphors shaping the international realm.

However, we need to qualify this approach: Policy makers--and I need to look at policy makers, because my argument is about how practice structures the international realm-- do not consistently apply general premises to the international system when developing new policies, as I argued in chapter 2. They do not argue that because the international system is an anarchical realm in which units interact analogously to the mechanistic laws of Newtonian physics, we cannot trust the U.N. or Saddam Hussein, or that not adhering to a specific international norm delegitimizes the language community which is at the basis of our thinking. Policy makers gain experience by dealing with contingent problems such as public diplomacy.

They do, however, bring background knowledge to the table, be it Kenneth Waltz's <u>Theory of International Politics</u> from their International Relations 101 class, or a newly fashionable concept, such as constructivism or Noopolitik (Wendt 1999; Arquilla, Ronfeldt 1999). They then relate their day-to-day experiences to such legitimating concepts.

Because of policy makers' reliance on such background scripts, it makes sense to focus systematically on how they conceptualize the international system on an abstract level. Because policy makers' concept of the international level impacts their actions, this type of abstract question is of great relevance.

One such conceptualization is that of John Arquilla and David Ronfeldt (1999). What is interesting in their approach is that they directly address policy makers and not academia. They talk of a knowledge realm, or noosphere.

The noosphere concept thus encompasses cyberspace and the info-sphere and has its own technological, organizational, and ideational levels. ...Few state or market actors, by themselves, seem likely to have much interest in fostering the construction of a global noosphere, except in limited areas having to do with international law, or political and economic ideology. The impetus for creating a global noosphere is more likely to emanate from activist NGOs, other civil-society actors (e.g., churches and schools), and private individuals dedicated to freedom of information and communications and to the spread of ethical values and norms.

If we accept such a background description for the international realm, it has ramifications for how we understand and practice politics in the international realm. Arquilla and Ronfeldt elaborate as follows: "Noopolitik is an approach to statecraft, to be undertaken as much by non-state as by state actors, that emphasizes the role of soft power in expressing ideas, values, norms, and ethics through all manner of media. This makes it distinct from realpolitik, which stresses the hard, material dimensions of power and treats states as the determinants of world order" (Arquilla and Ronfeldt 1999, 29).

By asking, "How do policy makers describe and legitimize public diplomacy?" we can also address the question, "Do policy makers describe the world in realpolitik or noopolitik terms?" and "What does this mean for how the U.S. conceptualizes global governance?" I am thereby able to generalize by arguing that if policy makers conceptualize public diplomacy as a language game and emphasize its importance, we can infer that they imagine a "noosphere." The trick is to focus on the policy level, where policy makers imagine the international realm, as opposed to the theory level of academics, in order to find out which ideas actually matter in the foreign policy process. In order to access the policy maker, offer them alternative world views, and hold them accountable, we need a philosophical-therapeutic approach (Chapter 4). Philosphical therapy focuses on the local dissolution of puzzlement of a policy maker through rational discourse between the policy maker and an interlocutor and is distinguished from a psycho-therapeutic approach in that it aims at rational misunderstandings, not personal idiosyncrasies. By analyzing the metaphors policy makers rely on and by therapeutically engaging them and forcing them to justify their actions in a specific situation, one can bring the politics behind the politics into the open (Chapter 3).

If paradigmatic change is taking place in international relations from realpolitik to noopolitik, hard power to soft power, or balance of power to global governance, it should manifest itself in public diplomacy.

The term *public diplomacy* only makes sense in a linguistic framework that allows for some type of truth discourse (Risse 2000). Therefore, we can look at the field as a type of early warning system that prepares us for the politics of paradigmatic change. By watching policy makers closely, we can identify when they aim to influence the paradigm and when they are themselves caught within a paradigm. Once we identify this, we can de-legitimize those actors that are relying on an argument of paradigmatic constraint in order to achieve their political aims, potentially free policy makers caught in the imagery of a paradigm, and offer policy alternatives.

To address these issues, I will look at the U.S.' so-called "War Against Terrorism." What is the role of public diplomacy for U.S. foreign policy in the campaign against terrorism? The Johnson-era need to win the "hearts and minds of the Arab population," seems to lead to foreign policies that lay greater emphasis on the political persuasion of foreign publics in order to build support for the acceptance of states' international actions.

Public diplomacy that is not epiphenomenal can only be conceptualized in a language-based framework connecting domestic and foreign policy. This means that a focus on public diplomacy is incompatible with hardcore structural-realist understandings of the world, assuming we accept the necessity of consistency, which policy makers do not have for the most part (chapter 2). I will show that the debate regarding the role of public diplomacy is not shaped by a discussion between the fundamentalists in both camps (realists or noospherists), but rather by pragmatic policy makers who are puzzled by their own misunderstanding of the concept and then revert to one of the more traditional frameworks. We will find that their focus is more on strategic influence than on developing a communicative realm.

Public Diplomacy and 9-11

Since the terrorist attacks on the World Trade Center in New York City, the debate on the role of public diplomacy has developed new urgency. President Bush stated at a press conference,

> "How do I respond, when I see that in some Islamic countries there is vitriolic hatred for America? I'll tell you how I respond: I'm amazed. I'm amazed that

there is such misunderstanding of what our country is about, that people would hate us. I am, I am -- like most Americans, I just can't believe it. Because I know how good we are, and we've got to do a better job of making our case."[55]

Jim Hoagland, Chief Foreign Correspondent at the <u>Washington Post</u>, argues in an interview, "Certainly in the Arab world and in the Muslim world, there's a feeling here in Washington that the U.S. did not get its message out promptly or effectively."[56] House International Relations Committee Chairman Henry Hyde asked at a recent congressional hearing,

> The poisonous image of the United States that is deliberately propagated around the world is more than a mere irritation. It has a direct and negative impact on American interests, not only by undermining our foreign policy goals but by endangering the safety of Americans here at home and abroad. How has this state of affairs come about? How is it, that the country that invented Hollywood and Madison Avenue has such trouble promoting a positive image of itself overseas?[57]

---

[55] Quoted in (Dumenco 2001).
[56] Interview with the BBC. It can be found at:
http://news.bbc.co.uk/hi/english/world/americas/newsid_1644000/1644
763.stm.
[57] Remarks of Henry J. Hyde Chairman, House International Relations
Committee, „The Role of Public Diplomacy in Support of the Anti-

Richard Holbrooke, former U.S. ambassador to the United Nations, describes the failure of U.S. public diplomacy in the fight against terrorism:

Examples abound: the military's strangely atonal radio message to the Afghans ("Attention Taliban! You are condemned. Did you know that? The instant the terrorists you support took over our planes, you sentenced yourself to death."), the failure to open a sustained public discussion with key Muslim intellectuals over how the Koran has been twisted by extremists into an endorsement of murder, he failure to publicize the fact that hundreds of those killed in the World Trade Center were Muslims, the failure to prove to Muslim women that their quest for progress and improved lives would be set back centuries by Bin Laden and his ilk, he failure to find credible Arabic-speaking Muslims to speak the truth about bin Laden.[58]

Tom Lantos stated before the House Committee on International Relations:

In many respects, ... the United States and our allies are losing the battle of the airwaves. We are literally being out-gunned, out-manned, and out-

---

Terrorist Campaign", October 10, 2001. The document can be found at: http://usinfo.state.gov/topical/pol/terror/01101017.htm
[58] Richard Holbrooke. "We must also win the battle for hearts and minds." Washington Post, Wednesday, October 31, 2001.

maneuvered on the public information battlefield. For years, the Taliban has showered Afghanistan with their hateful propaganda via Radio Shariat. These insidious messages echo throughout the Middle East and South Asia as fringe organizations and mainstream media alike spread their anti-American venom. The mass riots we see in the streets of Indonesia, Pakistan and other nations is proof positive that we are losing this aspect of the war.[59]

This puzzlement and self-indictment can partly be explained by the spirit of the general critical self-reflection on U.S. foreign policy in the aftermath of September 11. The unexpected nature of the attack by an unrecognized enemy has led to a general questioning of the merits of specific U.S. foreign policies. The intelligence community has been discussing the intrinsic worth of its technology-focused paradigm vs. more human intelligence. The general debate has reflected on the impact of September 11 on the Bush administration's "à la carte" multilateralism,[60] as well as on public diplomacy. In a corresponding matter to the multilateralism vs. unilateralism debate, political actors felt that they could rekindle their claims in the 'how should the U.S. sell itself' debate that had quieted down after the integration of USIA into the State Department.

---

[59] Representative Lantos' Statement on Fighting Terrorism at: http://usinfo.state.gov/topical/pol/terror/01101016.htm
[60] U.S. State Department Director for Policy Planning Richard Haas has coined the term "à la carte multilateralism."

On September 10, 2001, Colin Powell argued at the Coalition for American Leadership Abroad,

> Our public diplomacy efforts need to be expanded significantly to make this possible around the world. Our neglect of this area is evident in the negative image and criticism we receive in many nations. The decline of public diplomacy programs and other people-to-people exchanges that promote greater understanding of the U.S. has deteriorated. (For example, academic training sponsored by USAID is one-third of what it was ten years ago. Overall our exchange and cultural funding has declined in 2000 sharply from its1994 figure.) Our "voice" needs to be stronger and clearer.[61]

Preemptively answering Hyde's question, Charlie Brower, longtime chief executive officer of the advertising agency Batton, Barton, Durstine, and Osborn (BBDO), argued in the 1960s that the U.S. needed a sales force in the field to sell itself, "or we ought to stop asking why we can sell cornflakes and not democracy."[62] Although his is an interesting answer, it does not do justice to the complexity of the debate. It is an answer accepting the marketing analogy and offers a solution that is endogenous to that approach. I will show that the debate takes place on a more conceptual

---

[61] Collin Powell, Secretary of State, speaking on Diplomacy, September 10th 2001 at COLEAD 2001. The speech can be found at: colead.org.
[62] http://www.adage.com/news.cms?newsId=33340.

level and different metaphors are offered to deal with the problem.

Metaphors at Work: In Search of the Public Diplomacy Paradigm

It is interesting that in the case of public diplomacy, no single framework has been accepted as the mainstream paradigm, even though public diplomacy is an abstract practice, far from the material world (chapter 1). The term *public diplomacy*, i.e. communication between a state and a foreign public, is already theoretically laden. It reifies or even anthropomorphizes the state and its government, assigns communicative capacity to this entity and again reifies or anthropomorphizes the foreign public. It relies on a theory of domestic politics in which citizens influence national governments. It seems that by accepting the term *public diplomacy*, the discourse should already be structured and an initial framework outlined. The term in itself is therefore not undisputed and can conjure multiple definitions and policy actions.

Realpolitik Allows for Signaling-- Not Communication

A Waltzian realist framework of public diplomacy is logically impossible, since it would have to deny its own relevance (1979). However, strategically in a for-

150

eign policy debate where public diplomacy is on the agenda, even realists need to be able to say something about it. This realist paradigm, however, is still very much in vogue on the policy level. The conservatives around the Vice President Richard Cheney, not to be confused with the neo-conservatives around Paul Wolfowitz in the Bush administration, adhere to it. Realism conceptualizes public diplomacy as an epiphenomenon, a secondary phenomenon accompanying the interactions between states in the international system. It does neither harm nor good: The international system is structurally anarchic, in that there is no central source of global authority above the sovereign state. Therefore, the principal systemic source of order and outcomes in international politics is the distribution of material capabilities among nation states with unipolarity and U.S. hegemony as the central features of today's world. Realist literature has therefore not focused on international communication. Kenneth Waltz's Theory of International Politics (Waltz 1979) focuses purely on material capabilities which directly form the power basis of states and are used to increase states' security. For Waltz, there is a direct relationship between material objects (weapons) and future outcomes. Theory of International Politics, therefore, has two problems if utilized for an analysis of public diplomacy: it cannot conceptualize soft power (Nye 1990) or non-material factors (power of ideas, culture, etc.), and interests of states are assumed so narrowly (security maximization) that the systemic restraints of anarchy become so strong that state behavior can fully be explained by systemic factors. For such a theory, political communication to foreign publics is not only invisible, but even irrelevant. As a political concept it competes for legitimacy, attention of policy makers, and financial resources for its application. Realist-inspired policy makers, on the other hand, experience the importance of any concept competing with their favored paradigm. It is a major primary conceptual framework to categorize international relations and has great legitimizing power in the discourse on public diplomacy.

Stimulus-Response – Publics as Pavlovian Dogs

The *Pavlovian perspective*, a metaphor based on biological conditioning, conceptualizes public diplomacy as psychological operations (PSYOP) or psychological warfare (PSYWAR). *Psychological operations* may be defined broadly as the planned use of communications to influence human attitudes and behavior. The aim is to influence the behavior, emotions, and attitudes that support the attainment of national objectives. It utilizes any form of communication from word of mouth to the internet. It is based on a behavioristic understanding of human beings. Populations are conceptualized as actors that follow simple stimulus-response patterns (Skinner 1953). Through operant conditioning, reinforcement, and development understood as "learning", where one needs only the right methods to teach almost anything to anyone, PSYOP legitimizes its practices. Critique of the approach is either methodological, i.e. it does not describe reality well enough to be of use, or ideological, i.e. applying the approach reduces humanity's freedom of choice and right to self-determination. Lt. Col. Kenneth A. Turner of U.S. Army's 4th Psychological Operations Group at Fort Bragg, North Carolina, argues, "That's what we're all about: influencing people to take certain behavioral actions that accomplish our national goals."[63]

Main instruments for this type of public diplomacy are leaflets and radio broadcasts. In Afghanistan, with a population of 26 million, some 18 million leaflets have been distributed -- often via fiberglass "leaflet bombs" that explode in midair. "We have leaflets that are dropping like snowflakes in December in Chicago," Secretary of Defense Donald H. Rumsfeld noted earlier in the campaign.[64] The Commando Solo, or EC-130, planes have had some media attention in the war in Afghanistan. "Electrons, not bullets" is the motto of the 193rd Special Operations Wing of Harrisburg, Pennsylvania, which flies the radio stations. They obtain their mission taskings from the State Department. The U.S. Army's 4th

---

[63] Richard Leiby, "When Bombs Are Not Enough:The Army's Psyop Warriors Deploy an Arsenal of Paper," Washington Post December 10, 2001; Page C01.
[64] Richard Leiby, "When Bombs Are Not Enough:The Army's Psyop Warriors Deploy an Arsenal of Paper," Washington Post December 10, 2001; Page C01.

Psychological Operations Group produces messages for broadcasts. These messages are then assessed and approved by the State Department before being delivered to the 193rd Special Operations Wing. If the decision is for the message to be broadcast live rather than by taped message, a translator from the 4th PSYOP Group will be on the plane to broadcast the message in the language of the target audience. The messages range from the informative (color of cluster-bombs vs. color of food packages) to the propagandistic. The PSYOP framework in theory differentiates between dissemination of information and communication, which is conceptualized as a two-way discourse. However, for tactical and practical reasons the strategy focuses primarily on the dissemination of information. Arquilla and Ronfeldt (1999) agree with Murrow (chapter 2), "[f]irst, to have truly strategic (i.e., lasting) effect, initiatives in this area should be based on the truth. This is already a fundamental tenet of the American practice of psychological operations, as can be seen in Joint Publication 3-53, Doctrine for Psychological Operations." However, they qualify their argument, "[b]ut it must be noted that others have, in the past, found great value in the use of falsehoods—seeking strategic leverage through deception."

The PSYOP paradigm as a framework for public diplomacy is not considered as totalitarian and complementary to other communication activities, insofar that it sees itself as the military equivalent to a civilian approach. Its logic allows it to make a strict distinction between foreign publics as the target audience and the national public. However, it is heavily indebted to military thinking and it should not be forgotten that the power of the metaphor comes from its 'people as clay' image and the natural science legitimacy of the behavioral approach.

Propaganda: Political Economy of Communication

The propaganda framework is built on a perspective that public diplomacy disseminates special interests in order to secure their position in a mass society or world of mass societies. *Mass society* refers to the formal social structures that have supplanted traditional bonds with the industrial revolution; the formal contracts and bureaucratic institutions that replaced informal agreements; the urbanization that led to the demise of small, closely-knit communities; and the economic reasons that brought people together. The term is not theoretically innocent: it implies that social relationships of the past were more direct and thus more natural, thereby idealizing to an extent the prior social structures. Expanding social complexity increases the known world outside of the humans' immediate experience, which then increases the reliance on--and thereby the power of -- media. This, in turn, leads to theories that those who control the media therefore control mass society. This type of critique is based on a type of capture or conspiracy theory, i.e. special interests have captured the media in order to manage a population. It can also be based on a political economy approach, where self-reinforcing mechanisms automatically control the output of a medium, as Chomsky and Herrmann argue in <u>Manufacturing Consent: The Political Economy of The Mass Media</u>. Their propaganda model consists of five filters that sift out content that is not in the interest of the ruling class:

> (1) the size, concentrated ownership, ownership, owner wealth and profit orientation of the dominant mass-media firms; (2) advertising as the primary income source of the mass media; (3) the reliance of the media on information provided by government, business, and "experts" funded and approved by these primary sources and agents of power; (4) "flak" as a means of disciplining the media; and (5) "anticommunism" as a national religion and control mechanism. These elements interact with and reinforce one another. The raw material of news must pass through successive filters, leaving only the cleansed residue fit to print. They fix the premises of discourse and interpretation, and the definition of what is newsworthy in the first place, and they explain the basis and operations of what amount to propaganda and campaigns.

Notable about their approach is that they do not utilize a conspiracy theory but argue that media leaders do similar things because they see the world through similar lenses. The authors use the language of neoliberal economic theorizing, however, to make a (neo-)Marxist argument.

In <u>Deterring Democracy</u> (1993), Chomsky argues the status-quo critical approach prevalent in much of the writing on public diplomacy by the liberal and left-wing media. He argues that after the Cold War, politicians replaced fear of the Soviet Union with new threats in order to control public opinion, deflect attention from domestic problems, and maintain the illusion of democratic freedom.

This interest in a critical perspective on the role of communication in international relations is shared by a group of academics including James Der Derian, Edward Herrmann, and Nancy Snow, who have developed an impressive research program in the last twenty years which is often not noticed in the discipline of international relations, but popular among policy makers and critics of the United States.

Marketing USA: Branding vs. Selling

Metaphors taken from the realm of marketing have been with the public diplomacy debate since its inception. The traditional Madison Avenue metaphor is that of selling a product. The United States is hereby reified into a product with specific attributes, such as freedom of speech, individualism, multi-ethnicism, and Coca-Cola. As a marketer, USIA was responsible for ensuring that the advantages of

157

this product were made clear to its target audience. Secretary of State Colin Powell used this metaphor at the Net-Diplomacy Conference on September 6, 2001, when introducing former advertising agency CEO Charlotte Beers as the new Undersecretary for Public Diplomacy: "I wanted one of the world's greatest advertising experts, because what are we doing? We're selling. We're selling a product. That product we are selling is democracy. It's the free enterprise system, the American value system. It's a product very much in demand. It's a product that is very much needed."[65]

With the introduction of branding theory, the criticism of the product analogy has to a certain extent been answered. The idea of branding has gained prominence in the discourse on public diplomacy in the 1990s with the publication of Mark Leonard's book Britain™ (1997), Naomi Klein's book NO LOGO, and Peter van Ham's article in Foreign Affairs (2001), "The Rise of the Brand State." These concepts have been vigorously been debated in the Bush administration. Branding aims to create a holistic experience, correlating a company's products with a lifestyle or maybe even *Lebenswelt*. Peter van Ham (2001) develops the idea of the brand-state and argues that analogously to the development in marketing, where advertising gave way to branding, a similar paradigm shift is taking place in inter-

---

[65] U.S. Department of State, Office of the Spokesman September 6, 2001 Remarks by Secretary of State Collin Powell at the Netdiplomacy Conference, Department of State September 6, 2001. The speech can be found at: http://usembassy.state.gov/tokyo/wwwhse0306.html.

national relations. Advertising is aimed at increasing sales for a product by pointing out its advantages and increasing knowledge about it in the relevant sales channels. Branding is a paradigm shift insofar that the specific product becomes irrelevant because it only functions as carrier for the holistic brand experience. Ralph Lauren can sell sweaters, ties, and paint as long as the products are consistent with the yuppie-esque Ralph Lauren experience. A brand is diluted if it sells too many products that are inconsistent with its core normative beliefs. Peter van Hamm argues that a similar development is taking place in the realm of international relations. In an international system, in which states compete in attracting attention and making causal or normative claims, it becomes necessary to be branded, i.e. have a 'cool,' consistent (undiluted) and convincing image. Today, many policy makers use the language of marketing theory to describe their actions. Charlotte Beers, U.S. Undersecretary for Public Diplomacy and Public Affairs, argues, "The whole idea of building a brand is to create a relationship between the product and its user, ... We're going to have to communicate the intangible assets of the United States--things like our belief system and our values."[66] Elsewhere she argues in the same tone, "It is almost as though we have to redefine what America is.... This is the most sophisticated brand assignment I have ever had."[67]

---

[66] "Charlotte Beers' Toughest Sell: Can she market America to hostile Muslims abroad?" Business Week Online December 17, 2001.
[67] Richard Tomkins "Brand of the free." Financial Times, 20 October 2001.

Secretary of State Colin Powell explicitly distinguished between selling a product and branding last March, testifying before the House Budget Committee: "I'm going to be bringing people into the public diplomacy function of the department who are going to change from just selling us in the old USIA way to really branding foreign policy, branding the department, marketing the department, marketing American values to the world, and not just putting out pamphlets."[68]

The examples show that the vocabulary of marketing plays an important role in the public diplomacy strategy of the Bush administration. Arguments based on the branding metaphor seem to have great persuasive power. Jim Hoagland notes that the metaphor is not without critics. "The idea that putting out Madison Avenue techniques is going to solve the problem is going to be something that the astute American public is going to see through pretty quickly."[69]

William Rugh, the president of Amideast, a Washington D.C. organization that promotes understanding between the U.S. and the Middle East argues, "You can't boil down America into a slogan. America isn't a single product -- it's not Coca-Cola. If Charlotte Beers thinks America is a prod-

---

[68] Collin Powell at House Budget Committee March 15 (Unofficial Transcript).
[69] "US appoints terror war spin doctor," BBC News, Thursday, 8 November, 2001. The document can be found at:
http://news.bbc.co.uk/hi/english/world/americas/newsid_1644000/1644 763.stm

uct to sell, that won't work."[70] Specific actions by the State Department since September 11, 2001, can be categorized as indebted to brand management such as, (a) the reliance on polling, focus groups, and market segmentation, (b) the new focus on consistency and centralization in U.S. global communication, and (c) the tendency to ascribe a greater role to media of mass communication than to exchange programs.

However, the practice of public diplomacy in the Bush administration is not wholly guided by the metaphor. Foreign Service officers have not morphed into slick advertising agency executives and some observers argue that the day-to-day routine of U.S. public diplomacy is better described by the campaign metaphor.

The Campaign Metaphor

The campaign metaphor evokes the fast-paced media-cycle driven responses to the issue of political campaigns in U.S. presidential elections. Campaigns ideally or typically have a 'war room' where decisions to respond in 'real-time' are made by a committee. James Der Derian from Brown University describes this way of thinking in "The 9-11 Media Wars" (Der Derian 2001):

---

[70] Simon Dumenco "Stopping Spin Laden," <u>New York Magazine</u>. November 12, 2001.

The Pentagon's efforts were force-multiplied by the institution of a new White House media war room. Womaned by Karen P. Hughes, the White House communications director (and former Texas television reporter), Mary Matalin, chief political adviser to Vice President Dick Cheney (former television commentator), Charlotte Beers, the new Undersecretary of State for Public Diplomacy (former Madison Avenue advertising executive) and Victoria Clarke, chief Pentagon spokeswoman (former press secretary to George Bush senior), the war room was set up this week in the Indian Treaty Room of the Old Executive Office. Linked to London and Islamabad, its purpose is to present a 'message of the day' that will counter the chrono-geographic spin advantage enjoyed by the Taliban.

Referring to the inability of the U.S to respond to the false rumors in the Arabic world that the Israeli Mossad intelligence service was responsible for the attacks because thousands of Jews stayed home from their jobs in the World Trade Center that day, James Zogby, president of the Arab-American Institute, argues, "We are engaged in a political campaign. There needs to be a committee that reviews the Arab press every day and monitors Arab television. Seeds of problems must be confronted before they become issues."[71] Apart from the war room, there is a daily confer-

[71] Norman Kempster. "She Lands the Propaganda Account Diplomacy: President Bush is relying on a former Madison Avenue executive to

ence call among key staffers from the White House, the Defense Department, the State Department, and the British government. The whole operation is overseen by presidential counselor Karen Hughes, and managed by James Wilkinson, the White House Deputy Director of Communications for Planning. Mary Matalin argues:

> It is a kind of classic communications vehicle, doing classic things. The war room warriors' primary goal is to react quickly to false information put out by the enemy, rather than letting it hang out there in the long time-zone lag between Afghanistan and Washington. Typically, the Taliban, whatever happens, they take credit for it. We just got ahead of the story, so by the time the nets [news networks] had it... we knew what the right answer was.[72]

They also decide how to deploy top officials among media outlets, which are always hungry for talking heads in times of national crisis. Christopher Ross, the Arabic-speaking former U.S. ambassador to Syria, appeared on Al Jazeera for more than two hours, responding point by point to allegations made by the Taliban and Al Qaeda. Matalin argues that these quick-response media tactics have allowed the United States to gain the upper hand in the media cycle. "It's less airy, less Madison Avenue. This is just Campaign

---

persuade the Muslim world that the U.S. is not the enemy." New York Times, November 1, 2001.
[72] Richard Tomkins "Brand of the free." Financial Times, 20 October 2001.

101. Give them what makes sense to them. What makes sense to them is 'Islam is a peaceful religion.'... If you look at this in campaign terms -- and I'm loath to say this -- these are swing voters.[73]

The Newsroom Metaphor

The *newsroom metaphor* relies on the imagery of an independent press that aims to get as close to the truth as possible. It has been one way of legitimizing U.S. public diplomacy for a long time, even though it has always been criticized.

Lee McKnight, Associate Professor of International Communications at Tufts' Fletcher School argues in a <u>Boston Globe</u> article that regardless of the medium, any advertising message must be consistent with other U.S. diplomatic initiatives and impartial news programs broadcast to the region by U.S. agencies. He argues that the Kennedy administration was a good example for this type of approach. The well-known radio broadcaster Edward R. Murrow was in charge USIA at that time. Impartial newscasts, cultural exchanges, and Fulbright grants made up the context in which the U.S. government presented its views to

---

[73] Richard Tomkins "Brand of the free." <u>Financial Times</u>, 20 October 2001.

foreign publics, McKnight said: "It was crucial that news-casts were objective and instilled trust in the listeners. That was a big reason for appointing Murrow, whose whole reputation was based on independence. Over time, this strategy was successful and helped win the Cold War."[74] The Broadcasting Board of Governors (BBG) is the new home of all U.S. government and government-sponsored international broadcasting services. Marc B. Nathanson, the Chairman of the Board of the BBG, describes its mission:

> The mission of U.S. international broadcasting is to promote the open communication of information and ideas, in support of democracy, and the freedom to seek, receive, and impart information, worldwide. The mission of the BBG Board, of which I am the Chairman, is to ensure and safeguard the integrity, quality, and effectiveness of our international broad-casters. The role of U.S. international broadcasting today is as important as ever. It plays an important part in the broad support of democracy and the open exchange of accurate and objective news and ideas in countries and regions of the world where, because of geographic, developmental, or political reasons, there is a dearth of free and open information. U.S. international broadcasting empowers and educates. And in many cases, it is the only alternative voice.

---

[74] Chris Reidy. "Hearts, Minds, and Ads: Madison Avenue guru aims to discredit bin Laden by pitching US and freedom to young Muslims." Boston Globe, November 8, 2001.

The idea behind such an approach is either that an absolute congruence exists between U.S. interest and the "truth" according to global standards, or, more pragmatically, that in order to allow a conversation to take place between the U.S. government and foreign publics, it must be based on a set of common assumptions or truth discourse. Therefore the costs of lying or communicating untruthfully should be prohibitive.

Proponents of the newsroom metaphor argue that in addition to moral reasons, the disproportionate damage to the reputation of a media outlet if it is caught disseminating false information warrants extreme carefulness. This is especially important if one accepts the inherent bias by parts of the media that governments in general disseminate untruthful propaganda and therefore monitor them carefully.

Critics of the newsroom metaphor argue that public diplomacy is the strategic dissemination of information and therefore misrepresented if it compares itself to the independent media. In the Reagan administration and in neoconservative circles of the Bush administration, the idea of influencing foreign publics with whatever means necessary has its adherents (chapter 2). More fundamental critics, such as the propaganda theorists, of course criticize the conception of the independent media itself.

The Field Trip Metaphor

Scholars and policy makers adhering to the field trip metaphor argue that only total immersion, personal experience, and direct intercultural communication can enable foreign publics to understand the United States. Programs subscribing to this theory include the Fulbright Exchange Program and the International Visitor Program (IVP). The International Visitor Program of the U.S. Department of State annually brings to the United States approximately 5,000 foreign nationals from all over the world to meet and confer with their professional counterparts and to experience America firsthand. The visitors, who are selected by American Foreign Service Officers overseas, are current or potential leaders in government, politics, the media, education, labor relations, the arts, business and other fields. Among the thousands of distinguished individuals who have participated in the International Visitor Program since its inception more than five decades ago are more than 186 current and former Chiefs of State, 1500 cabinet-level ministers, and many other distinguished leaders from the public and private sectors.[75]

The implicit assumption in this case is that if somebody experiences life in the United States, he or she will view the country and its foreign policy positively. Critics point out that knowing and liking a country are separate processes, as can be seen in the example of the terrorists of September 11, several of whom had lived in the U.S. for quite some time.

---

[75] http://exchanges.state.gov/education/ivp/index.htm.

The State of the Policy Level Debate

An analysis of the metaphors policy makers use in order to describe, explain, and legitimize the practice of public diplomacy after September 11 has shown that substantial differences exist in how policy makers view public diplomacy. Policy makers agree that disparate programs such as student exchanges, broadcasting, and press spokespersons should be categorized as public diplomacy. Depending on where policy makers are situated on the scale between realpolitik and a global village, they will use different metaphors to describe public diplomacy's thrust. Confusion arises when policy makers are caught up in powerful metaphors that cannot easily be integrated, like the "War Against Terrorism," branding, and the field trip. The metaphors policy makers use to frame their arguments in the discourse on public diplomacy have not coalesced. It actually seems that there is unbridgeable tension between truth-based approaches and instrumental approaches. However, because public diplomacy is an abstract practice, metaphors they rely on determine to a large extent the types of actual policies they support.

In order to categorize the metaphors policy makers use into the 'grand' base metaphors of chapter 3, I categorize these metaphors. At a first glance this seems problematic, because now we are subsuming metaphors under metaphors. Following Fauconnier's (1997) argument that our thinking is permeated by metaphors, we can categorize them as on different levels of abstraction from the perspective of the observer. The framework includes three main ways of distinguishing between the presented metaphors.

A first perspective is to make the distinction between *dissemination of information* and *communication,* where dissemination allows for one-way information flows, while communication allows for a two-way communication flow. This is an interesting typology, where *selling, propaganda,* the *newsroom* could be conceptualized as dissemination, while *branding* and *the field trip* could be conceptualized as communication. However, the approach pays no attention to interesting linguistic questions that need to be addressed if we want to generalize from the issue area of public diplomacy to more general U.S. foreign policy making.

A second perspective is to focus on the *conceptualization of foreign publics,* the essential aspect of the metaphorical approach. *Selling, campaign,* and the *newsroom* metaphors accept the other as rational actors that need to be persuaded by information that-- truthful or not-- is taken into account by the uninformed foreign public.

Branding, field trip, propaganda, and *PSYOP* rely on a concept of foreign publics as moldable psyches that can be influenced in the interest-formation phase. Interest-formation is endogenous to the approach.

A third, and for the question of how U.S. foreign policy conceptualizes global governance, most important perspective focuses on the *language theory* necessary in order to allow the metaphor to be plausible. The *realpolitik approach* needs no common language between the government and the foreign publics, and the *newsroom metaphor, the propa-*

169

ganda model, selling, and branding need foreign publics that give a government the benefit of the doubt that it might be disseminating the truth, while only the *PSYOP* approach needs almost no such sphere, as long as it can influence directly.

If all conceptualizations of the abstract practice of public diplomacy rely on some type of language community and public diplomacy is becoming more important, can this be read as an indicator that the U.S. foreign policy is changing from realpolitik to noopolitik? With the debate about the formation of an Office of Strategic Influence and a White House Office for Global Diplomacy, it seems that noopolitik has indeed gone mainstream.

However, it is interesting how a world language community is conceptualized in which these offices take up their work. In the following paragraphs, I extrapolate not from the practice of these institutions, but from what policy makers claim they will be doing.

By focusing on the strategic aspect of communication, policy makers accept a world communicative sphere as a background condition. However, they do not lay emphasis on nurturing this communicative realm, but on instrumentalizing this discourse in order to persuade.

It leads to the question of how the U.S. political system, that on the inside values the communicative realm absolutely, pursues such a Machiavellian approach in the international realm. If we distinguish between the international and the national realms, a noosphere is not possible. This might seem sensible, because the international system is still full of Machiavellian fiefdoms. However, in a globalizing world we need to ask ourselves, "What are the criteria that would allow the U.S. to recognize that the outside is similar enough so that participation in a global communicative discourse is possible?"

Basically, it should be easy. We can imagine a world without language and community, a world where we do not trust anybody, discount everything they say, and take only information we gather from their action as signaling their true intentions. This is -- for strange historical reasons -- called realism, or realpolitik. Alternately, we could accept that a world community exists where we can do things with words (Austin 1962). The viability of what someone says in such a world would be measured in something that we call trust. Trust is increased over time if the truth is spoken and decreases when lies are told and pointed at. In such a world, public diplomacy could do two things: It could either aim to influence strategically, by telling lies, or build trust by telling the truth. Public Diplomacy is communication. Therefore, only if we believe that some type of global village exists should we care about it. If we do so, however, then trust matters, and we need to monitor our trust levels carefully.

Therefore, in order to further the political project of noopolitik, we need to take a step back and look at the pre-scientific metaphors that shape the way we see the world and our position in it. Public diplomacy is an interesting indicator showing how these changes are taking place. It shows that in a globalizing world it is time to politicize our thinking about thinking.

Conclusion: Unearthing the Politics of Globalization

In chapter six, I sum up my findings and conclude that the developments outlined in the preceding chapters need to be addressed by political science. A critical perspective is necessary, in order to unearth the politics of globalization.

What I did

I posed the question, "What is the role of public diplomacy in a globalizing world?" and tried to address it. Let me recount: I started out by observing that it is impossible to talk about public diplomacy, a phenomenon based on international communication, without a critical reevaluation of some of the basic assumptions of conventional policy sciences. I also remarked that there are inconsistencies between the real world and our perceptions of it, inconsistencies increased by the process of transformative change the world is currently undergoing, and which is generally called *globalization*. Therefore I reformulated the question into: "How can we, on a conceptual level, describe and access the politics that are taking place in this time of transformative change?" In this situation *policy makers*, i.e. anyone responsible for shaping political contexts by imagining scenarios, structuring expectations, or actually making decisions, are therefore involved in politics on a more fundamental level than usual. The disconnection between the images in our heads and the real world during transformative change decreases the ability of policy makers and principals to identify potentially political situations where choice is possible. Policy makers run the risk of missing out on chances to take political decisions and offer alternative perspectives. Their principals might miss out on the chance to hold them accountable for their actions.

Since these developments challenge conventional political theory and its tools, we need a new vocabulary to describe these types of problems. Furthermore, due to the interdependence of policy making and theorizing, we need a model of how the two interact. Sketching two discourses with different criteria of validity and different aims enabled me to focus my inquiry on the epistemic level.

Metaphorology allows us to prove that the imagination of policy makers is, even on an epistemic level, a political issue. Philosophical therapy offers a technique to interact with the policy maker on this level in order to free the policy maker and make him accountable to his principals.

By introducing metaphorology and philosophical therapy, I offered methods that can unearth the political moves that prestructure later policy processes and show how much of what is politically interesting has already been decided by selecting one image over another -- independently of whether this decision is made consciously or not.

A metaphorological approach is the right type of critical approach, because our world is getting ever more abstract: we are farther away from material entities, and we are submerged in imagery. In other words, the role of metaphors in guiding our politics is increasing. A metaphorological approach thus allows us to push back the envelope to where intuition rules (chapter 1). Political concepts, as elaborate as they may be, are always based on foundational metaphors carrying implicit assumptions. Philosophical therapy lets us deal with contexts that have become depoliticized; we believe that we have less ability to influence the design of our collectivities than we actually do.

Looking at how images influence our thinking, there does not seem to be an alternative to metaphorology, and in dealing with individual angst of giving up familiar imagery, some type of therapeutic approach is necessary. It is debatable whether a psychological therapeutic approach should be preferred to a philosophical therapeutic approach, although even if it could potentially address local problems of individual policy makers, it would not allow us to assign responsibility to their action and make them accountable to their principals. Our approach would then be empathetic, not political.

Vocabulary

Any text that introduces vocabulary from outside the discipline has to defend this choice. Therefore, some reflection is necessary. Most of the terms I employ are self-explanatory and come from the discipline of philosophy of science, which offers the appropriate vocabulary for my type of inquiry. Since we are not dealing with conventional international relations vocabulary, it makes sense at this point to summarize the individual terms and concepts.

In chapters one and three, I distinguished between the *theory level*, the reflective level of the academic discipline focusing on an issue, and the *policy level*, the level where empirical action takes place and where the social aspects of the world are imagined. This distinction is interesting, not because policy makers naturally take part in theoretical discussions and academics take part on the policy level, but because it allows us to situate the political moment of imagining the world at the policy level. By unearthing this political realm with the help of metaphorology, the reflection about the base metaphors that prestructure our worlds, we can assist policy makers in realizing the political aspects of their decision for a certain base metaphor, and by uncovering this process through the technique of philosophical therapy we can increase accountability by enabling their principals to challenge the policy makers' views of the world. I defined policy makers as actors who 'create' the world by persuading their principals to accept a certain description of it, and by then acting according to the consequences their description implies. *Principals* was used as the generic term for the individuals and groups that policy makers represent, as in principal-agent theorizing. This relationship between principal and policy maker was defined as legal, moral, or political. The term politics therefore was defined as decision making by policy makers, via their imagining communities and their worlds, and by persuading principals within these imagined worlds and communities of the necessity a of certain perspectives or actions.

Public diplomacy is a subject that lends itself naturally to this type of thinking because it is an abstract practice, a concept that only makes sense and becomes of strategic interest if policy makers share highly generalized assumptions on how the world is prestructured. Public Diplomacy is not a very popular field of political science research because the mainstream base metaphor in international relations, the Hobbesian state of nature, is not able to provide adequate vocabulary - the exclusion of communication is in fact its theoretical keystone.

I use the terms *globalizing world* and *transformative change* interchangeably. My inquiry rests on the assumption that transformative change is actually taking place, and that therefore we need to reflect upon our basic understandings of the world. I defined uncovering/recovering the political realm as the act of (a) increasing the freedom of policy makers to reach decisions by pointing out to them that they have choices in contexts where they believe to be constrained by necessity, and (b) to hold policy makers accountable to their principles and thereby empower their principals.

Even if my assumption of transformative change were wrong, the damage my project could cause would be limited. If there were no global change, philosophical therapy would not succeed, and policy makers, our interlocutors, would stick to their perspective of the world, and no harm would be done.

I describe philosophical therapy as a perspective and a technique. As a perspective it offers the ability to focus on local problems, to interact with an interlocutor, and to increase freedom and assign responsibility. As a technique, I describe it as a four-step procedure, where we need to challenge a dogma, expose a picture that stands behind this dogma, propose an alternative picture of concept-application, and deflect anxiety about the new way of seeing the world.

A Plea for a Critical Perspective

The question remains if this type of inquiry is interesting for the problem of dealing with the role of communicating foreign policy only, or if it might have wider relevance. I argue it is relevant beyond this particular case. In fact, I argue that in times of transformative change, when many of the most important aspects of politics take place on the level where we imagine our worlds, asking these types of questions becomes political.

If we accept the relevance of critical political science during times of transformative change, and if we assume that we are in fact in a time of transformative change, new responsibilities follow for the political scientist. The traditional metaphor of the political scientist as a natural scientist who has factual knowledge, who can break down complexity and offer rational or technocratic solutions to the policy maker becomes contested.

This inquiry has shown that in times when we experience change in our world views and a disconnection between our approaches and empirical experience exists, we need critical tools that can deal with the policy makers' personal anxiety.

As political scientists we must move closer to the policy maker, and, without being co-opted into a political project, work therapeutically with our clients, introducing the frame of mind of metaphorology and applying the technique of philosophical therapy.

Bibliography

Alexandre, Laurien. The Voice of America: From Detente to the Reagan Doctrine. Norwood, NJ: Ablex, 1988.

Allison, Graham and Philip Zelikow. Essence of Decision : Explaining the Cuban Missile Crisis. Reading, MA: Longman, 1999.

Anderson, Benedict, Imagined Communities: Reflections on the Origin and Spread of Nationalism, Revised Edition, New York: Verso, 1991.

Andrea, Alfred J. and James H. Overfield, eds.. The Human Record: Sources of Global History , Vol. II. Boston: Houghton Mifflin, 1994.

Aristotle, The Complete Works of Aristotle: The revised Oxford Translation. J. Barnes ed. 2 vols. Princeton, 1984.

Arquilla, John and David Ronfeldt. Emergence of Noopolitik Toward an American Information Strategy. Santa Monica, CA: RAND, 1999.

Arquilla, John and David Ronfeldt. Networks and Netwars: The Future of Terror, Crime, and Militancy. Santa Monica, Calif.: RAND, 2001.

Arquilla, John, and David Ronfeldt, eds. In Athena's Camp: Preparing for Conflict in the Information Age. Santa Monica, Calif.: RAND, 1997.

Arquilla, John, and David Ronfeldt, The Advent of Netwar. Santa Monica, Calif.RAND, 1996.

Austin, J.L. How To Do Things with Words. Cambridge: Harvard University Press, 1962.

Axelrod, Robert and Michael D. Cohen, Harnessing Complexity: Organizational Implications of a Scientific Frontier. Free Press, 2000.

Axelrod, Robert, The Evolution of Cooperation. New York: Basic Books, 1984.

Axelrod, Robert. The Complexity of Cooperation. Princeton, NJ: Princeton University Press, 1997.

Baker, Gordon P. and Peter M.S. Hacker, Wittgenstein: Rules, Grammar and Necessity (volume 2 of "An Analytic commentary on the Philosophical Investigations") Oxford, Oxford University Press, 1985.

Baker, Gordon. Wittgenstein on Metaphysical / Everyday Use. Oxford, unpublished manuscript, 2000.

Baldwin, David, ed. Neorealism and Neoliberalism : The Contemporary Debate. New York : Columbia University Press, 1993.

Balfe, Judith Huggins. "Artworks as Symbols in International Politics." International Journal of Politics, Culture and Society 1.2 (Winter 1987): 527.

Barber, Benjamin. Jihad Vs. McWorld. New York: Basic Books, 1995.

Bartelson, Jens. A Genealogy of Sovereignty. Cambridge: Cambridge University Press, 1995.

Baudrillard, Jean. <u>Simulacra and Simulation</u>. Trans. Sheila Faria Glaser. Ann Arbor : University of Michigan Press, 1999.

Bauman, Zygmunt. <u>Globalization: The Human Consequences</u>. New York: Columbia University Press, 1998.

Baxter, Laurence, and Jo Ann Bishop. "Uncharted Ground: Canada, Middle Power Leadership, and Public Diplomacy." <u>Journal of Public and International Affairs</u> 9 (1998): 84101.

Beniger, James R. "Theoretical Perspectives Toward and Old New Paradigms: The Half-Century Flirtation With Mass Society." <u>Public Opinion Quarterly</u>, 51.2: Supplement 50th Anniversary Issue. (1987): S46-S66.

Beniger, James R., <u>The Control Revolution: Technological and Economic Origins of the Information Society</u>. Cambridge, Mass.: Harvard University Press, 1986.

Berners-Lee, Tim and Mark Fischetti <u>Weaving the Web : The Original Design and Ultimate Destiny of the World Wide Web by its Inventor</u>. San Francisco: Harpers, 1999.

Blumenberg, Hans: <u>Paradigmen zu einer Metaphorologie</u>. Frankfurt am Main: Suhrkamp, 1999.

Broadie, Sarah and Christopher Rowe ed. <u>Aristotle: Nicomachean Ethics - Translation, Introduction, Commentary</u>. Oxford. Oxford University Press, 2002.

Brown, John. "The Purposes and Cross-Purposes of American Public Diplomacy." <u>American Diplomacy</u>, August 2002.

Bull, Hedley, <u>The Anarchical Society, A Study of Order in World Politics</u>. New York: Columbia University Press, 1977.

Buzan, Barry. "The Level of Analysis Problem in International Relations Reconsidered," in Ken Booth and Steve Smith, eds., International Relations Theory Today. Oxford: Oxford University Press, 1995.

Cameron G. Thies. "Progress, History and Identity in International Relations Theory : The Case of the Idealist- Realist Debate." <u>European Journal for International Relations</u> 2002.

Carothers, Thomas. <u>Aiding Democracy Abroad, The Learning Curve</u>. Washington, DC: Carnegie Endowment for International Peace, 1999.

Castells, Manuel. The <u>Rise of the Network Society, The Information Age: Economy, Society and Culture, Vol. I</u>. Oxford: Blackwell, 1996.

Cederman, Lars-Eric. <u>Emergent actors in world politics : how states and nations develop and dissolve</u>. Princeton, NJ: Princeton University Press, 1997.

Cherrington, Ben M. A Personal Reminiscence: 1926-1951. Denver: Social Science Foundation,1973.

Chomsky, Noam [US] Power in the global arena. New Left Review 230, July/August 1998: 327.

Chomsky, Noam. Deterring Democracy. New York: Hill and Wang, 1993.

Christensen, Thomas J. and Jack Snyder, "Chain Gangs and Passed Bucks: Predicting Alliance Patterns in Multipolarity." International Organization 44:2. Spring 1990, pp. 137-168.

Codignola, Luca (ed.). Guide to Documents Relating to French and British North America in the Archives of the Sacred Congregation "de Propaganda Fide" in Rome, 1622-1799. Ottawa: National Archives of Canada, 1991.

Cooper, Jr., John Milton, Breaking the Heart of the World Woodrow Wilson and the Fight for the League of Nations. Cambridge University Press: Cambridge, 2001.

Cox, Kevin, ed. Spaces of Globalization : Reasserting the Power of the Local. New York: Guilford Books, 1997.

Creel, George. How we advertised America; the first telling of the amazing story of the Committee on the public information that carried the gospel of Americanism to every corner of the globe. New York: Harper & brothers, 1920.

Dahl, Robert. A Preface to Democratic Theory. Chicago: University of Chicago Press, 1956.

Della Porta, Donatella, and Mario Diani. Social movements : an introduction. Oxford: Blackwell, 1999.

Der Derian, James and Michael J. Shapiro, eds. International/Intertextual Relations: Postmodern Readings in World Politics. Lexington: Lexington Books, 1989.

Der Derian, James. „9.11: The Media Wars." INFOinterventions. November 11, 2001.

Descartes, René. Meditations on first philosophy; translated by John Cottington. Cambridge University Press: New York, 1996.

Dizard, Wilson Jr. Digital Diplomacy: U.S. Foreign Policy in the Information Age. Westport, CT: Praeger, 2001.

Dizard, Wilson. The Strategy of Truth: The Story of the United States Information Service. Washington, 1961.

Drake, William. The New Information Infrastructure : Strategies for U.S. Policy. Washington D.C.: Brookings Institution Press, 1995.

Dumenco, Simon. "Stopping Spin Laden." New York Magazine. November 12, 2001.

Eckstein, Harry. "Case Study and Theory in Political Science," in Fred I. Greenstein and Nelson W. Polsby, eds., Handbook of Political Science, Volume 7:

Strategies of Inquiry. New York: Addison-Wesley, 1975.

Einstein, Albert. Relativity: The Special and the General Theory. Trans. Robert W. Lawson. 1916; reprint New York: Bonanza Books, 1952.

Espinosa, J. Manuel. Inter-American Beginnings of U.S. Cultural Diplomacy, 1938-1948. Washington, 1976.

Fauconnier, Gilles. Mappings in Thought and Language, Cambridge: Cambridge University Press, 1997.

Feyerabend, Paul: Against Method. New York: Verso Press, 1991.

Foucault, Michel. The Archaeology of Knowledge and the Discourse on Language. A. M. Sheridan Smith, translator. New York: Pantheon, 1972.

Freedom House. Comparative Survey of Freedom. Washington DC: Freedom House, 1999.

Freud, Sigmund. Vorlesungen zur Einführung in die Psychoanalyse. Frankfurt: Fischer, 1991.

Friedman, Thomas L. The Lexus and the Olive Tree: Understanding Globalization. New York: Farrar, Straus and Giroux, 1999.

Fukuyama, Francis, The End of History and the Last Man. New York: Free Press, 1992.

Geiger, Gebhard. „Neue Strukturen und Herausforderungen der internationales Sicherheit im Informationszeitalter." Aussenpolitik 48 (4), 1997: 401408.

Gibson, John S. "Public Diplomacy: Public-Private Cooperation to Represent the United States to the World" International Educator, Volume VII, No. 2-3, Spring 1998.

Giddens, Anthony. The Constitution of Society. Polity Press, 1984.

Giddens, Anthony: Runaway World: How Globalisation is reshaping our lives. London: Profile Books, 1999.

Gilboa, Eytan. Media diplomacy. Conceptual divergence and applications. Harvard International Journal of Press/Politics 3 (3), Summer 1998: 5675.

Gladwell, M. The Tipping Point: How little things make can make a big difference. New York: Little Brown, 2000.

Gleick, James. Chaos: Making a New Science. New York: Penguin, 1987.

Gore, Albert Jr. From Red Tape to Results: Creating a Government That Works Better & Costs Less. New York, 2001.

Grant, Robert T., and Reeve, Basil: Observations on the General Effects of Injury in Man: With Special Reference to Wound Shock. London: Medical Research Council, Special Report No. 277, 1944.

Haas, Ernst B. "The Balance of Power: Prescription, Concept, or Propaganda?" World Politics 5:4 (July 1953), pp. 442-477.

Habermas, Jürgen: „Von der Konstitutions- zur Kommunikationstheorie der Gesellschaft (Sellars und Wittgenstein). Kommunikativer und kognitiver Gebrauch der Sprache." Vorstudien und Ergänzungen zur Theorie des kommunikativen Handelns. Frankfurt: Suhrkamp,1984.

Hacker, Peter M. S. Wittgenstein. London: Routledge, 1999.

Ham, Peter Van. The Rise of the Brand State: The Postmodern Politics of Image and Reputation, Foreign Affairs, 80 (5): (September/October 2001) 2-6

Held, David and Anthony McGraw.: The Global Transformations Reader: An Introduction to the Globalization Debate. Malden, Mass: Polity Press, 2000.

Held, David. Democracy and the Global Order: From the Modern State to Cosmopolitan Governance. Stanford: Stanford Univ. Press. 1995.

Herman, Edward and Noam Chomsky. Manufacturing consent: the political economy of the mass media. New York: Pantheon Books, 1988.

Hirsch, Michael. "Bush and the World." Foreign Affairs, 81 (5): (September/October 2002).

Hirst, Paul, and Grahame Thompson. Globalization in Question. Cambridge: Polity Press, 1996.

Hixson, Walter L. Parting the Curtain: Propaganda, Culture and the Cold War. New York, 1977.

Hobbes, Thomas. Leviathan. ed. by J.C.A. Gaskin. Oxford: Oxford University Press, 1998.

Hutchings, Robert (ed.). At the end of the American century : America's role in the postcold war world. Baltimore : Johns Hopkins University Press, 1998.

Jahn, Beate. The Cultural Construction of International Relations : The Invention of the State of Nature, Basingstoke: Palgrave, 2000.

Jervis, Robert "Cooperation Under the Security Dilemma." World Politics 30:2. January 1978, pp. 167-214.

Jervis, Robert. System Effects: Complexity in Political and Social Life. Princeton: Princeton University Press, 1997.

Kant, Immanuel. Werke in sechs Bänden. Rolf Toman ed. Cologne: Könemann, 1995.

Kaplan, Robert D. The Coming Anarchy. New York: Random House, 2000.

Kaplan, Robert D., Warrior politics : why leadership demands a pagan ethos. New York: Random House, 2002.

Keck, Margaret E. and Kathryn Sikkink. <u>Activist Beyond Borders: Advocacy Networks in International Politics</u>. Ithaca: Cornell University Press, 1998.

Kelly, Kevin. <u>New Rules for the New Economy</u>. New York: Viking Press, 1998.

Kennan, George F. "The Sources of Soviet Conduct", <u>Foreign Affairs</u> 25 (1947), pp. 566-82.

Keohane, Robert and Joseph S. Nye Jr. "Power and Interdependence Reconsidered," <u>International Organization</u> 41(Fall 1987).

Keohane, Robert ed., <u>Neorealism and Its Critics</u>. New York: Columbia University Press, 1986.

Keohane, Robert O. <u>After Hegemony: Cooperation and Discord in the World Political Economy</u>. Princeton: Princeton University Press, 1984.

Keynes, John Maynard. <u>General Theory of Employment, Interest and Money</u>. London: Macmillan, 1936.

King, Gary, Robert O. Keohane, and Sidney Verba. <u>Designing Social Inquiry: Scientific Inference in Qualitative Research</u>. Princeton: Princeton University Press, 1994.

Klein, Naomi. <u>No Logo</u>. New York: St. Martin's Press, 1999.

Kratochwil, Friedrich. <u>Rules, Norms, and Decisions: On the conditions of practical and legal reasoning in international relations and domestic affairs</u>. Cambridge. Cambridge University Press. 1989.

Kuhn, Thomas. The Structure of Scientific Revolutions, 2d. enlarged ed. Chicago, Illinois: The University of Chicago Press, 1970.

Lakatos and Musgrave, eds., Criticism and the Growth of Knowledge. Cambridge University Press, 1970.

Lakoff, George and Mark Johnson. Philosophy in the flesh: the embodied mind and its challenge to Western thought. New York: Basic Books, 1999.

Lakoff, George, and Mark Johnson, Metaphors We Live By, Chicago: The University of Chicago Press, 1980.

Lapid, Yosef. "The Third Debate: On the Prospects of International Theory in a Post-Positivist Era." International Studies Quarterly 33(3) (September 1989): 235-254.

Lasswell, Harold D. Propaganda Technique in the World War. New York: Peter Smith, 1938.

Lasswell, Harold Dwight, Propaganda and promotional activities, an annotated bibliography, prepared under the direction of the Advisory committee on pressure groups and propaganda, Social science research council [by] Harold D. Lasswell, Ralph D. Casey [and] Bruce Lannes Smith. Minneapolis, The University of Minnesota press, 1935.

Lazarsfeld, Paul F. Growth of a Theory: Public Opinion and the Classical Tradition Public Opinion Quarterly, Vol. 21, No. 1. Spring, 1957, pp. 39-53.

Lebow, Richard Ned. "Beyond Parsimony : Rethinking Theories of Coercive Bargaining." European Journal for International Relations. Volume 4 Issue 1 (March 1998), 31.

Leonard, Mark. Britain TM. London: Demos, 1997.

Leonard, Mark. Public Diplomacy. London: Demos, 2002.

Lichello, Robert. Edward R. Murrow, Broadcaster of Courage. Charlottesville, New York: SamHar Press, 1971.

Linklater, Andrew. "The Achievements of Critical Theory." In International Theory: Positivism and Beyond, edited by Steve Smith, Ken Booth and Marysia Zalewski, 279-298. Cambridge: Cambridge University Press, 1996.

Lippman, Walther. Public Opinion. New York: Harcourt Brace-Carey, 1922.

Livy, The Rise of Rome, Books 1-5, tr. T.J. Luce. Oxford: Oxford University Press, 1998.

Lovelock, James E. Gaia. Oxford: Oxford University Press 1979.

Machiavelli, Niccolò. The Prince and the Discourses. New York: Random House, 1940.

MacIntyre, Alasdair. A Short History of Ethics, 2nd ed., University of Notre Dame Press, 1998.

Malone, Gifford D. Political Advocacy and Cultural Communication: Organizing the Nation's Public Diplomacy. Lanham, MD, 1988.

Maturana H.R. and Varela F.G. The Tree of Knowledge, revised edition. Boston: Shambhala, 1992.

McLuhan, Marshall: Understanding Media. New York: McGraw-Hill Media, 1964.

Mearsheimer, John J. "The False Promise of International Institutions." International Security 19:3 (Winter 1994/95), pp. 5-49.

Meyer, John. „World Society and the Nation State." with J. Boli, G. Thomas, and F. Ramirez. American Journal of Sociology 103 (1997): 144-81.

Miller, Dennis. "Storming the Palace in Political Science: Scholars join revolt against the domination of mathematical approaches to the discipline." The Chronicle of Higher Education. September 21, 2001.

Miller, Steven E., "The End of Unilateralism or Unilateralism Redux?" The Washington Quarterly (Winter 2002) 25 (1)

Milner, Helen. Interests, institutions, and information : domestic politics and international relations. Princeton, N.J. : Princeton University Press, 1997.

Mock, James R. and Cedric Larson. Words that Won the War: The Story of the Committee on Public Information, 1917-1919. Princeton, Princeton University Press,1939.

Morgenthau, Hans J., and Kenneth Thompson 5th ed. <u>Politics among nations: the struggle for power and peace</u>. New York : Alfred A. Knopf, 1985.

Naisbitt, John. <u>Global Paradox</u>. New York: William Morrow and Company, 1994.

Negroponte, Nicholas. "Being Wireless." <u>Wired Magazine</u>. October 2002.

Neufeld, Mark. <u>Restructuring of International Relations Theory</u>. Cambridge: Cambridge University Press, 1995.

Newton, Isaac. <u>Newton's Philosophy of Nature: Selections from His Writings</u>, H.S. Thayer, ed., New York, 1953.

Nietzsche, Friedrich. <u>Sämtliche Werke, Kritische Studienausgabe.</u> Giorgio Colli and Mazzino Montinari ed. Munich: München: de Gruyter / dtv, new edition 1999.

Ninkovich, Frank A. <u>The Diplomacy of Ideas: U.S. Foreign Policy and Cultural Relations, 1938-1950</u>. Cambridge: Cambridge University Press, 1981.

Ninkovich, Frank. <u>U.S. Information Policy and Cultural Diplomacy</u>. New York, NY: Praeger 1996.

Norris, Pippa ed. <u>Critical citizens : global support for democratic government.</u> New York : Oxford University Press, 1999.

Nye, Joseph S. Jr., The Paradox of American Power: Why the World's Only Superpower Can't Go It Alone, Oxford University Press, 2002.

Nye, Joseph S., and William A. Owens, "America's Information Edge," Foreign Affairs, Vol. 75, No. 2, March/April 1996, pp. 20–36.

Nye, Joseph S., Bound to Lead: The Changing Nature of American Power. New York: Basic Books, 1990.

O'Hefferman, P. Mass Media and American Foreign Policy. Norwood, N.J.: Ablex, 1991.

Ohmae, Kenichi, The End of the Nation-State: The Rise of Regional Economies. New York: The Free Press, 1995.

Parker, B. Evolution and revolution: from international business to Globalization. In S.R. Clegg, C. Hardy & W.R. Nord eds. Handbook of organization studies. London: Sage. 1996.

Perry, William J. "The Pentagon and the Press," Harvard International Journal of Press/Politics 1 (1), Winter 1996

Peter A. Gourevitch, "Robert O. Keohane: The Study of International Relations." Political Science and Politics, September 1999.

Potter, Evan H. ed. Cyber-Diplomacy: Managing Foreign Policy in the Twenty-First Century. Ottawa: McGill-Queen's University Press, 2002.

Rawls, John. A Theory of Justice. Cambridge, MA: Harvard University Press, 1971.

Reinicke, Wolfgang H. Global Public Policy. Washington DC: Brookings Institution, 1998.

Reinicke, Wolfgang H.. „Global Public Policy." Foreign Affairs (November/ December, 1997).

Risse, Thomas "Let's argue!": Communicative action in world politics" International Organization (54) Winter 2000.

Rorty, Richard ed. The Linguistic Turn: Recent Essays in Philosophical Method. Chicago, Chicago University Press, 1967.

Rosenau, James N. "Distant Proximities: The Dynamics and Dialectics of Globalization." In International Political Economy: Understanding Global Disorder, edited by Björn Hettne, 46-64. London: Zed Books, 1995.

Rosenau, James N. Along the Domestic-Foreign Frontier. Exploring Governance in a Turbulent World. Cambridge: Cambridge University Press ,1997.

Ross, Steven. The economic theory of agency: The principal's problem. American Economic Review, 63(2) 1973: 134-139.

Rushdie, Salman. Haroun and the Sea of Stories. New York: Penguin, 1990.

Ryan, Frederick J. ed. Ronald Reagan: The Great Communicator. New York: Harper, 2001.

Sahtouris, Elisabet "The Biology of Globalization.". Perspectives in Business and Social Change, September 1997.

Samuelson, Paul A. and William D. Nordhaus. Economics, 15th ed. New York: McGraw-Hill, 1995.

Sassen, Saskia. Globalization and Its Discontents, New York: The New Press, 1998.

Sassen, Saskia. Losing Control: Sovereignty in an Age of Globalization. New York: Columbia University Press. 1996.

Saunders, Frances Stonor Who Paid the Piper?: The CIA and the Cultural Cold War. London, Routledge, 1999.

Schelling, Thomas C. The Strategy of Conflict. Cambridge, MA: Harvard University Press, 1980.

Schiller, Herbert and Kaarle Nordenstreng (eds.). Beyond national sovereignty : international communication in the 1990s. Norwood, NJ : Ablex Pub. Co., 1993.

Schiller, Herbert. Communication and cultural domination. White Plains, N.Y.: International Arts and Sciences Press, 1976.

Shy, Oz. The Economics of Network Industries. Cambridge: Cambridge University Press, 2001.

Simma, Bruno and Andreas Paulus "The International Community: Facing the Challenge of Globalization.". Peace Res. Abstracts 38, no. 2 (2001): 274.

Singer, J. David. "The Level-of-Analysis Problem in International Relations," in Klaus Knorr and Sidney Verba, eds., The International System: Theoretical Essays. Princeton, N.J.: Princeton University Press, 1961.

Skinner, B. F. Science and human behavior. New York: Macmillan, 1953.

Smith, Steve. "Positivism and Beyond." In International Theory: Positivism and Beyond, edited by Steve Smith, Ken Booth and Marysia Zalewski, 11-44. Cambridge: Cambridge University Press, 1996.

Snidal, Duncan. "Relative Gains and the Pattern of International Cooperation." American Political Science Review 85(3) (1991): 701-726.

Snow, Nancy E. "United States Information Agency," Foreign Policy in Focus, Volume 2, Number 40 August 1997.

Snyder, Alvin. Warriors of disinformation : American propaganda, Soviet lies, and the winning of the Cold War, an insider's account. New York: Arcade Pub. 1995.

Sorensen, Thomas C. The Word War: The Story of American Propaganda. New York, 1968.

Spence, M. and R. Zeckhauser. "Insurance, information and individual action." American Economic Review 61(2) 1971: 380-387.

Stimson Center, The Henry L. The Project for the Advocacy of US Interests Abroad. Equipped for the Future: Managing US Foreign Affairs in the 21st Century. Washington: Stimson Center, 1998.

Strange, Susan. States and Markets. 2nd ed. London and Washington: Pinter, 1994.

Tuch, Hans N. Communicating with the World: U.S. Public Diplomacy Overseas. New York: St Martin's Press,1990.

Turner, Henry A. Woodrow Wilson and Public Opinion. Public Opinion Quarterly, Vol. 21, No. 4. (Winter, 1957-1958), pp. 505-520.

US Advisory Commission on Public Diplomacy. A New Diplomacy for the Information Age. Washington: US Advisory Commission on Public Diplomacy, 1996.

US Advisory Commission on Public Diplomacy. Publics and Diplomats in the Global Communications Age. Washington: US Advisory Commission on Public Diplomacy, 1998.

Waismann Friedrich: How I see Philosophy. London. Macmillan. 1968.

Walker, Robert B. J. Inside/outside: International Relations as Political Theory. Cambridge: Cambridge University Press, 1993.

Wallerstein, Immanuel. The End of the World As We Know It: Social Science for the Twenty-First Century. Minneapolis: University of Minnesota Press, 1999.

Walt, Stephen M. "Beyond bin Laden: Reshaping U.S Foreign Policy." International Security (Winter 2001/2002) 26

Walt, Stephen M. „Beyond bin Laden: Reshaping U.S. Foreign Policy" International Security. Vol. 26. No. 3. Winter 2002. pp 56 – 78.

Waltz, Kenneth N. Man, the State, and War: A Theoretical Analysis. New York: Columbia University Press,1954.

Waltz, Kenneth N. Theory of International Politics. New York: McGraw-Hill, 1979.

Watzlawick, Paul ed. The Invented Reality. New York: Norton, 1984.

Weaver, Ole. "The rise and fall of the inter-paradigm debate" in Steve Smith, Ken Booth, and Marysia Zalewski eds. International Theory: Positivism and Beyond. Cambridge University Press, Cambridge, 1996.

Weber, Max. Politik als Beruf. Stuttgart: Reclam, 1992.

Weber, Max: Wirtschaft und Gesellschaft. 5. Aufl. Tübingen: Mohr, 1974.

Webster's Third New International Dictionary, Cologne: Köneman, 1993.

Wendt, Alexander. Social Theory of International Politics. Cambridge: Cambridge University Press, 1999.

Wendt, Alexander. Social Theory of International Politics. Cambridge: Cambridge University Press, 1999.

Wilson, Woodrow. An Address in Washington to the League to Enforce Peace. May 27, 1916.

Winkler, Allan M. The Politics of Propaganda: The Office of War Information, 1942-1945. New Haven, Yale University Press, 1978.

Wittgenstein, Ludwig. Philosophische Untersuchungen, Philosophical Investigations 2nd ed. Oxford: Basil Blackwell, 1958.

Wittgenstein, Ludwig. Volume II of the Philosophical Grammar. ed. R. Rhees, trs. A. Kenny, Blackwell 1969, p. 194.

Wohlstetter, Albert. "The Delicate Balance of Terror." P-1472, Santa Monica: RAND, 1958.

Woods, Randall B. Fulbright: A Biography. New York: Cambridge University Press, 1995.

Zacher, Mark W. and Brent A. Sutton. Governing Global Networks: International Regimes for Transportation and Communication. Cambridge: Cambridge University Press, 1995.

Zalewski, Marysia. "All these theories yet the bodies keep piling up: Theories, Theorists and Theorising." in Steve Smith, Ken Booth, and Marysia Zalewski eds. <u>International Theory: Positivism and Beyond</u>. Cambridge University Press: Cambridge, 1996.

Fragen politischer Ordnung in einer globalisierten Welt
herausgegeben von Prof. Dr. Friedrich Kratochwil
(Universität München)

Alexander Mutschler
Eine Frage der Herrschaft
Betrachtungen zum Problem des Staatszerfalls in Afrika am Beispiel Äthiopiens und Somalias
Insbesondere in Staaten der sog. Dritten Welt kommt es immer wieder zu Fällen von Staatszerfall, die im Extremfall, wie etwa in Somalia, zum Verschwinden von staatlichen Strukturen führen. In dieser Arbeit wird Staatszerfall mit Hilfe politischer Begriffe und Faktoren analysiert. Zum einen wird nach der Funktionalität und Legitimität der Herrschaft des Staates, zum anderen nach der Rolle von in Konkurrenz zum Staat stehender Herrschaftsverbände gefragt. Vor diesem Hintergrund wird in zwei Fallstudien, Äthiopien und Somalia, die Entwicklung dieser Staaten seit Ende des zweiten Weltkriegs bis zum Niedergang der Militärdiktaturen zu Beginn der 90er Jahre betrachtet.
Bd. 1, 2002, 360 S., 25,90 €, br., ISBN 3-8258-6138-4

Doris A. Fuchs; Friedrich Kratochwil (eds.)
Transformative Change and Global Order
Reflections on Theory and Practice
The world at the beginning of the 21st century is fundamentally different from what it was only 50 years ago – or so it seems. In the political realm, scholars identify deep changes in organization. What are the new institutions and qualities of political order? Debates on this question have focused on two concepts in particular: globalization and global governance. Using these concepts as entrance points, therefore, the contributors to this volume explore theory and practice of political organization in a transformed/ing world with the aim of shaping the post-globalization discussion.
Bd. 2, 2002, 272 S., 20,90 €, br., ISBN 3-8258-6374-3

Wissenschaftliche Paperbacks
Politikwissenschaft

Hartmut Elsenhans
Das Internationale System zwischen Zivilgesellschaft und Rente
Gegen derzeitige Theorieangebote für die Erklärung der Ursachen und die Auswirkungen wachsender transnationaler und internationaler Verflechtung setzt das hier vorliegende Konzept eine stark durch politökonomische Überlegungen integrierte Perspektive, die auf politologischen, soziologischen, ökonomischen und philosophischen Ansatzpunkten aufbaut. Mit diesem Konzept soll gezeigt werden, daß der durch Produktionsauslagerungen/Direktinvestitionen/neue Muster der internationalen Arbeitsteilung gekennzeichnete (im weiteren als Transnationalisierung von Wirtschaftsbeziehungen bezeichnete) kapitalistische Impuls zur Integration der bisher nicht in die Weltwirtschaft voll integrierten Peripherie weiterhin zu schwach ist, als daß dort nichtmarktwirtschaftliche Formen der Aneignung von Überschuß entscheidend zurückgedrängt werden können. Das sich herausbildende internationale System ist deshalb durch miteinander verschränkte Strukturen von Markt- und Nichtmarktökonomie gekennzeichnet, die nur unter bestimmten Voraussetzungen synergetische Effekte in Richtung einer autonomen und zivilisierten Weltzivilgesellschaft entfalten werden. Dabei treten neue Strukturen von Nichtmarktökonomie auf transnationaler Ebene auf, während der Wiederaufstieg von Renten der zivilgesellschaftlichen Grundlagen funktionierender oder potentiell zu Funktionsfähigkeit zu bringender, dann kapitalistischer Systeme auf internationaler und lokaler Ebene eher behindert.
Bd. 6, 2001, 140 S., 12,90 €, br., ISBN 3-8258-4837-x

Klaus Schubert
Innovation und Ordnung
In einer evolutionär voranschreitenden Welt sind statische Politikmodelle und -theorien problematisch. Deshalb lohnt es sich, die wichtigste Quelle für die Entstehung der policy-analysis, den Pragmatismus, als dynamische, demokratieendogene politisch-philosophische Strömung zu rekonstruieren. Dies geschieht im ersten Teil der Studie. Der zweite Teil trägt zum Verständnis des daraus folgenden politikwissenschaftlichen Ansatzes bei. Darüber hinaus wird durch eine konstruktiv-spekulative Argumentation versucht, die z.Z. wenig innovative Theorie- und Methodendiskussion in der Politikwissenschaft anzuregen.
Bd. 7, 2003, 224 S., 25,90 €, br., ISBN 3-8258-6091-4

Politik: Forschung und Wissenschaft

Klaus Segbers; Kerstin Imbusch (eds.)
The Globalization of Eastern Europe
Teaching International Relations Without Borders
Bd. 1, 2000, 600 S., 35,90 €, br., ISBN 3-8258-4729-2

LIT Verlag Münster – Hamburg – Berlin – London
Grevener Str./Fresnostr. 2 48159 Münster
Tel.: 0251 – 23 50 91 – Fax: 0251 – 23 19 72
e-Mail: vertrieb@lit-verlag.de – http://www.lit-verlag.de

Hartwig Hummel; Ulrich Menzel (Hg.)
Die Ethnisierung internationaler Wirtschaftsbeziehungen und daraus resultierende Konflikte
Mit Beiträgen von Annabelle Gambe,
Hartwig Hummel, Ulrich Menzel
und Birgit Wehrhöfer
Bd. 2, 2001, 272 S., 30,90 €, br., ISBN 3-8258-4836-1

Theodor Ebert
Opponieren und Regieren mit gewaltfreien Mitteln
Pazifismus – Grundsätze und Erfahrungen für das 21. Jahrhundert. Band 1
Bd. 3, 2001, 328 S., 20,90 €, br., ISBN 3-8258-5706-9

Theodor Ebert
Der Kosovo-Krieg aus pazifistischer Sicht
Pazifismus – Grundsätze und Erfahrungen für das 21. Jahrhundert. Band 2
Bd. 4, 2001, 176 S., 12,90 €, br., ISBN 3-8258-5707-7

Wolfgang Gieler
Handbuch der Ausländer- und Zuwanderungspolitik
Von Afghanistan bis Zypern
In der Literatur zur Ausländer- und Zuwanderungspolitik fehlt ein Handbuch, dass einen schnellen und kompakten Überblick dieses Politikbereichs ermöglicht. Das vorliegende Handbuch bemüht sich diese wissenschaftliche Lücke zu schließen. Thematisiert werden die Ausländer- und Zuwanderungspolitik weltweiter Staaten von Afghanistan bis Zypern. Zentrale Fragestellung ist dabei der Umgang mit Fremden, das heißt mit Nicht-Inländern im jeweiligen Staat. Hierbei werden insbesondere politische, soziale, rechtliche, wirtschaftliche und kulturelle Aspekte mitberücksichtigt. Um eine Kompatibilität der Beiträge herzustellen beinhaltet jeder Beitrag darüber hinaus eine Zusammenstellung der historischen Grunddaten und eine Tabelle zur jeweiligen Anzahl der im Staat lebenden Ausländer. Die vorgelegte Publikation versteht sich als ein grundlegendes Nachschlagewerk. Neben dem universitären Bereich richtet es sich besonders an die gesellschaftspolitisch interessierte Öffentlichkeit und den auf sozialwissenschaftlichen Kenntnissen angewiesenen Personen in Politik, Verwaltung, Medien, Bildungseinrichtungen und Migranten-Organisationen.
Bd. 6, 2003, 768 S., 98,90 €, gb., ISBN 3-8258-6444-8

Friedensgutachten
der Hessischen Stiftung für Friedens- und Konfliktforschung (HSFK), des Bonn International Center for Conversion (BICC), des Instituts für Entwicklung und Frieden (INEF), der Forschungsstätte der Evangelischen Studiengemeinschaft (FEST), des Instituts für Friedensforschung und Sicherheitspolitik an der Universität Hamburg (IFSH)

Friedensgutachten 2003
herausgegeben von Corinna Hauswedell, Christoph Weller, Ulrich Ratsch, Reinhard Mutz, Bruno Schoch
Das Friedensgutachten 2003 stellt die Frage nach der Zukunft von Kooperation oder Konfrontation in der neuen Weltordnung. Die weitreichenden Folgen des 11. September 2001 und der Krieg gegen den Irak haben nicht nur die transatlantischen Beziehungen und die Zusammenarbeit in den internationalen Institutionen erschüttert, sie machen die tiefer gehenden Asymmetrien des neuen Weltgefüges sichtbar: Das Verhältnis von Macht und Recht in den internationalen Beziehungen steht auf dem Prüfstand; Militarisierung bedroht Entwicklung, Gerechtigkeit, Demokratie und humane Wertesysteme. Auf der Basis einer Analyse dieser grundlegenden Tendenzen fragen die Autoren nach den Auswirkungen und Alternativen in relevanten Weltregionen, für das Nord-Süd-Verhältnis und nach der zukünftigen Rolle Europas: Wie soll eine Friedensordnung im Mittleren Osten Gestalt gewinnen, im Irak, zwischen Israel und Palästina, im zerrissenen Afghanistan? Wie können sich die Konfliktregionen Afrikas aus der Umklammerung von Gewaltökonomien und Plünderung ihrer Ressourcen befreien? Welche Bedrohung geht von Nordkorea aus? Was bedeutet der globale Anti-Terrorkrieg für Südostasien oder Kolumbien? Wie müssen die Instrumente globaler Ordnung, des Völkerrechts und der UNO weiterentwickelt werden?
Das Friedensgutachten wird im Auftrag der fünf Institute herausgegeben von Corinna Hauswedell, Christoph Weller, Ulrich Ratsch, Reinhard Mutz und Bruno Schoch. Es kostet 12,90 Euro, im Abonnement 8,50 Euro.
2003, 336 S., 12,90 €, br., ISBN 3-8258-6760-9

LIT Verlag Münster – Hamburg – Berlin – London
Grevener Str./Fresnostr. 2 48159 Münster
Tel.: 0251 – 23 50 91 – Fax: 0251 – 23 19 72
e-Mail: vertrieb@lit-verlag.de – http://www.lit-verlag.de

Münchener Beiträge zur Geschichte und Gegenwart der internationalen Politik

herausgegeben von Peter J. Opitz
unter Mitwirkung von Mir A. Ferdowski
und Dietmar Herz

Günter Kast
Der schwierige Abschied von der Vorherrschaft
Die Vereinigten Staaten von Amerika und die neue internationale Ordnung im asiatisch-pazifischen Raum

Die Vereinigten Staaten von Amerika schmücken sich seit dem Zerfall des sowjetischen Imperiums mit dem Prädikat "einzige verbliebene Supermacht". Diesen Titel kann den USA derzeit keine Nation streitig machen, zumal die potentiellen Herausforderer aus dem asiatisch-pazifischen Raum infolge der Währungs- und Finanzkrise ihre Aufholjagd bis auf weiteres verschieben mußten. Dieser Befund darf jedoch nicht darüber hinweg täuschen, daß das Machtgefälle zwischen Washington und seinen pazifischen Nachbarn langfristig betrachtet abnehmen wird. Insbesondere China – von der asiatischen "Grippe" bisher unbeeindruckt – wird im 21. Jahrhundert seinen Einfluß als regionale Ordnungsmacht verstärkt geltend machen. Parallel dazu nimmt in Fernost die Bereitschaft ab, die USA als Hegemonialmacht zu akzeptieren. Es entsteht stattdessen ein multipolares Staatensystem – ein strategisches Viereck, in dem neben den Vereinigten Staaten auch China, Japan und Rußland eine Hauptrolle spielen werden. Die USA dürfen diesen evolutionären Prozeß hin zu einem von Institutionen unterfütterten Mächtegleichgewicht nicht blockieren, wenn dieser friedlich verlaufen soll. Insbesondere die US-Militärpräsenz in Japan und Südkorea wird von den immer selbstbewußter auftretenden Nationen Ostasiens zunehmend als Anachronismus wahrgenommen, der nur deshalb noch stillschweigend toleriert wird, weil es keine gangbare Alternative zu geben scheint. Die vorliegende Studie soll dazu beitragen, diese "Denkblockaden" aufzuheben. Es wird ein Design für eine neue Sicherheitsarchitektur entworfen, das in nicht allzu ferner Zeit auf die Forderung hinausläuft: "Ami, go home!"
Bd. 7, 1998, 296 S., 25,90 €, br., ISBN 3-8258-3876-5

Claudius Rosenthal
Zur Legitimation von Außenpolitik durch Politische Theorie
Wie läßt sich Außenpolitik legitimieren? Der Autor beantwortet diese nach 1989 besonders aktuelle Frage unter Verweis auf die Politische Theorie:

Nicht Tradition, nicht Gesetze, nicht charismatische Führer und nicht der Verweis auf ein höchstes Ziel, sondern vornehmlich das "systematisierte Argument" könnten der heutigen Außenpolitik Legitimation verschaffen. Den Nachweis für diese These führt der Autor zunächst begründungstheoretisch; er entwickelt dann Kategorien, mit denen sich das Legitimationspotential unterschiedlicher Politischer Theorien bestimmen läßt.
Bd. 8, 2001, 570 S., 40,90 €, br., ISBN 3-8258-4840-x

Heike Schröder
Negotiating the Kyoto Protocol
An analysis of negotiation dynamics in international negotiations

Climate change has become an important policy area, one which has been gaining momentum since the adoption of the Kyoto Protocol in December 1997. The Kyoto Protocol was adopted by 159 nations after a tenacious final marathon of negotiations, during which all unresolved issues were hammered out one by one. The commitments that were finally agreed upon exceeded the original expectations. Despite its shortcomings, the Kyoto Protocol is a constructive compromise worthy of commendation, and is therefore a remarkable diplomatic achievement. The aim of this book is not only to present an introduction to the historical, legal and political foundations of the Kyoto Protocol, but also to offer a thorough analysis of the negotiation process at the Kyoto Conference. It investigates the positions, interests and strategies of three crucial players, the EU, US and Japan, on the issue of climate change and examines how these influenced the outcome of the negotiations. Furthermore, it examines the impact of other factors on the final result. This book thus presents a unique case study of an international negotiation process, negotiation strategies and conference dynamics. It is an indispensable guide for political scientists, policy makers, negotiators and all those interested in negotiation processes and the politics of climate change.
Bd. 9, 2001, 208 S., 20,90 €, br., ISBN 3-8258-5446-9

Berliner Studien zur Internationalen Politik

herausgegeben von Dr. Werner Pfennig
(Freie Universität Berlin)

Daniel Haas
Mit Sozialklauseln gegen Kinderarbeit?
Das Beispiel der indischen Teppichproduktion
Das Thema "Sozialklauseln in internationalen Handelsverträgen" – seit dem Abschluß der

LIT Verlag Münster – Hamburg – Berlin – London
Grevener Str./Fresnostr. 2 48159 Münster
Tel.: 0251 – 23 50 91 – Fax: 0251 – 23 19 72
e-Mail: vertrieb@lit-verlag.de – http://www.lit-verlag.de

Uruguay-Runde des *Allgemeinen Zoll- und Handelsabkommens* (GATT) wieder verstärkt in der Diskussion – steht im Spannungsfeld von Handels- und Entwicklungspolitik und muß im Kontext ungehemmter ökonomischer Globalisierung betrachtet werden. Können Sozialklauseln ein Regulativ für den sozial (und ökologisch) außer Rand und Band geratenen Weltmarkt sein? Können Sozialklauseln das entwicklungspolitische Instrumentarium zur Durchsetzung sozialer Mindeststandards sinnvoll ergänzen? Die vorliegende Arbeit betrachtet die Sozialklausel-Idee aus der Sicht eines Entwicklungslandes und richtet den Blick besonders auf die für die massive Ausbeutung von Kindern berüchtigte indische Teppichexportproduktion. Es werden konkrete Umsetzungsprobleme einer – wie auch immer gearteten – Verknüpfung des Zugangs zu internationalen Märkten mit der Einhaltung sozialer Mindeststandards in Exportbetrieben beleuchtet und Chancen sowie Risiken einer solchen Verknüpfung am vorliegenden Fall kritisch analysiert. Zu guter Letzt faßt der Autor die Reaktionen und Argumentationslinien von indischen Basisbewegungen, Gewerkschaftern und Regierungsvertretern zusammen und greift dabei auf reichhaltiges empirisches Material sowie eigene Interviews zurück.

Bd. 4, 1998, 152 S., 20,90 €, br., ISBN 3-8258-3583-9

Sebastian Bersick
ASEM: Eine neue Qualität der Kooperation zwischen Europa und Asien
Das Asia-Europa Meeting (ASEM) ist in den zwei Jahren seines Bestehens zu einem zentralen Mechanismus der Zusammenarbeit zwischen Europa und Asien geworden. Parallel zur der bisherigen interregionalen Kooperation im Rahmen des EU-ASEAN-Dialogs sind innerhalb des ASEM-Prozesses, neben den Staaten der ASEAN, ebenso Japan, die Republik Korea und die Volksrepublik China Teilnehmer einer weiteren interregionalen Kooperationsinitiative. Gegenstand dieser Arbeit sind Genese und Entfaltung des ASEM-Prozesses sowie die Interessen, die von den beteiligten Akteuren verfolgt werden. Im Mittelpunkt der Analyse steht die Frage, ob und inwieweit das ASEM eine neue Form der Kooperation hervorgebracht hat und daher der europoäisch-asiatischen Zusammenarbeit eine neue Qualität verleiht. Mit dieser Untersuchung liegt die erste deutschsprachige Monographie über den ASEM-Prozeß vor, der jüngsten und zugleich ambitioniertesten Initiative innerhalb der europäisch-asiatischen Beziehungen.

Bd. 5, 1999, 128 S., 15,90 €, br., ISBN 3-8258-4173-1

Udoy M. Ghose
Die Transformation der Indischen Union
Eine empirische und theoretische Analyse der Wirtschaftsreformen 1991 – 96 und ihrer Implikationen für die Mainstream Transformationstheorie
Mehr als 40 Jahre lang verfolgte Indien eine von starken planwirtschaftlichen Elementen geprägte Wirtschaftspolitik. Erst mit dem Antritt der Regierung unter Premierminister Rao wurde die Marktwirtschaft zur ökonomischen Leitlinie erhoben. Theoretische Grundlage dafür war (und ist) die „Mainstream"-Transformationstheorie neoklassischer Provenienz, mit der sich diese Arbeit kritisch auseinandersetzt und zudem das Fundament für eine empirisch gehaltvolle Theorie der Transformation legt. Indiens Transformationsprozeß in der entscheidenden Phase 1991 – 96 liefert dafür das empirische Material.

Bd. 6, 2003, 288 S., 20,90 €, br., ISBN 3-8258-6631-9

Thomas Benedikter
Krieg im Himalaya
Hintergründe des Maoistenaufstandes in Nepal. Eine politische Landeskunde
2002 war das blutigste Jahr in der Geschichte Nepals seit dem Krieg gegen die Briten 1815/16. Im Land herrscht Ausnahmezustand und ohne Rücksicht auf die Zivilbevölkerung geht die Armee ohne Rücksicht auf die Zivilbevölkerung gegen die maoistische Volksbefreiungsarmee vor. Diese startet von ihren Basisgebieten aus Großangriffe auf Militärstützpunkte und trägt ihre Guerrilla immer mehr in die Städte. Nach 7 Jahren „Volkskrieg" mit fast 7.500 Toten nimmt, unbeachtet von der Weltöffentlichkeit, die Dynamik von Gewalt und Vergeltung ihren scheinbar unaufhaltsamen Lauf....
Wie konnte es so weit kommen? Was wollen die Maoisten? Was hat zu diesem Konflikt geführt? Der Autor hat 2002 verschiedene Schauplätze des Maoistenaufstandes besucht und monatelang in Kathmandu recherchiert. Er geht nicht nur auf die Maoistenbewegung und deren Aufstand ein, sondern hellt auch die wichtigsten sozialen und politischen Aspekte Nepals auf, die den Hintergrund dieses Konfliktes bilden. Das reich illustrierte Buch geht vom aktuellen Geschehen aus, ist aber vor allem eine politische Landeskunde des heutigen Nepal.

Bd. 7, 2003, 264 S., 19,90 €, br., ISBN 3-8258-6895-8

LIT Verlag Münster – Hamburg – Berlin – London
Grevener Str./Fresnostr. 2 48159 Münster
Tel.: 0251 – 23 50 91 – Fax: 0251 – 23 19 72
e-Mail: vertrieb@lit-verlag.de – http://www.lit-verlag.de

Regensburger Schriften zur Auswärtigen Politik

herausgegeben von Prof. Dr. Stephan Bierling
(Universität Regensburg)

Robert Kulzer
Demokratieverständnis und demokratische Praxis des African National Congress (1994–1999)
Mit den ersten freien Wahlen vom April 1994 ist die Befreiungsbewegung African National Congress (ANC) zur bestimmenden Regierungspartei in Südafrika geworden. Aufgrund des überwältigenden Rückhaltes in der schwarzen Bevölkerung wird der ANC die politische Zukunft des Landes auf absehbare Zeit maßgeblich gestalten. Vom ANC hängt es ab, wie – und ob – sich die junge und ungefestigte Demokratie in Südafrika entwickeln wird.
Die Analyse der ersten fünf Regierungsjahre des ANC zeichnet nicht nur anhand konkreter Entwicklungen den Umgang des ANC mit demokratischen Institutionen nach und zeigt damit die demokratische Praxis des ANC als Partei und als Regierung auf, sondern sie erschließt aus dem Handeln, aber vor allem aus den Aussagen und Dokumenten des ANC auch dessen theoretisches Demokratieverständnis. Im Ergebnis wird deutlich, dass die zentrale Stellung des ANC sehr wohl ein Risiko für die Entwicklung der Demokratie in Südafrika darstellt.
Bd. 1, 2001, 192 S., 25,90 €, br., ISBN 3-8258-5131-1

Hans-Joachim Bauer
Der Europarat nach der Zeitenwende 1989–1999
Zur Rolle Straßburgs im gesamteuropäischen Integrationsprozeß
Bei seiner Gründung im Jahr 1949 stand der Europarat im Zentrum der europäischen Zusammenarbeit und Integration. In den darauffolgenden Jahrzehnten liefen ihm jedoch andere Organisationen den Rang ab. Ein Schattendasein war die Folge. Erst mit dem Zusammenbruch des Ostblocks und dem Ende der Spaltung Europas Ende der achziger und in den neunziger Jahren rückte Straßburg wiederum verstärkt in den Blickpunkt der europäischen Politik. Die Studie untersucht, welche Rolle der Europarat in den Jahren zwischen 1989 und 1999 spielte und ob er den – nicht zuletzt von seiten der mittel- und osteuropäischen Reformstaaten in ihn gesetzten – hochgesteckten Erwartungen gerecht werden konnte. Im Mittelpunkt der Analyse steht dabei die Osterweiterung der Straßburger Organisation, die zu einer problematischen Aufweichung ihrer für den Kontinent so wichtigen Prinzipien geführt hat. Außerdem wird das Verhältnis Straßburgs zu EU und OSZE beleuchtet, das von sektoraler Doppelarbeit und mangelnder Abstimmung geprägt ist.
Bd. 2, 2001, 368 S., 25,90 €, br., ISBN 3-8258-5178-8

Dorothea Lamatsch
Euro versus Dollar
Die währungspolitische Integration Europas aus US-amerikanischer Perspektive 1969–1999
"Wake up, America!" – mit dieser Aufforderung versuchten Wissenschaftler die Aufmerksamkeit der Amerikaner auf die währungspolitischen Aktivitäten der Europäischen Union zu lenken. Die Einführung des Euro im Jahr 1999 markierte den vorläufigen Höhepunkt einer 30-jährigen Entwicklung in Europa. Aber auch die Handelspartner, allen voran die USA, sind von den Folgen dieses Schritts betroffen. Manche Auguren sagten sogar das Ende der Dollar-Hegemonie voraus. Das vorliegende Buch analysiert, wie die US-Administrationen seit 1969 – begleitet von stürmischen internationalen Währungsbeziehungen – die Entwicklung hin zur Einheitswährung verfolgt haben.
Bd. 3, 2002, 240 S., 17,90 €, br., ISBN 3-8258-5946-0

Texte zu Politik und Zeitgeschichte

herausgegeben von Hans Karl Rupp
(Universität Marburg)

Wolfgang Hecker; Joachim Klein; Hans Karl Rupp (Hg.)
Politik und Wissenschaft. 50 Jahre Politikwissenschaft in Marburg
Band 1: Zur Geschichte des Instituts
Die Marburger Politikwissenschaft ist bekannt – ihre Geschichte weniger. Der erste Band dieser Festschrift zum 50-jährigen Jubiläum zeichnet die Entwicklung des Fachs und der Institution nach: Von der Berufung Wolfgang Abendroths 1951, den Jürgen Habermas treffend als "Partisanenprofessor im Lande der Mitläufer" charakterisierte, über die Phase der Revolte und Hochschulreform (End-60er und 70er Jahre) bis hin zur "Professionalisierung" ab den 80er Jahren.
Ganz im Unterschied zu gängigen (Vor-)Urteilen ist die Geschichte der Marburger Politikwissenschaft vielschichtig, von Kontroversen, aber auch von hohem wissenschaftlichen Output geprägt. Und sie ist spannend zu lesen. Kenntnisreich und kompetent dargestellt von ehemaligen und derzeit Lehrenden.
Im Mai 2001 wird ein Symposium kritische Bilanz ziehen und Perspektiven für die Marburger Politikwissenschaft diskutieren.
Bd. 1, 2001, 408 S., 25,90 €, br., ISBN 3-8258-5440-x

LIT Verlag Münster – Hamburg – Berlin – London
Grevener Str./Fresnostr. 2 48159 Münster
Tel.: 0251 – 23 50 91 – Fax: 0251 – 23 19 72
e-Mail: vertrieb@lit-verlag.de – http://www.lit-verlag.de

A. Kai-Uwe Lange
George Frost Kennan und der Kalte Krieg
Eine Analyse der Kennanschen Variante der
Containment Policy
George F. Kennan, entscheidender Ideengeber
für die strategische Konzeption des Marshallpla-
nes, wird in diesem Buch als Stratege des Kalten
Krieges erkannt, der mit einer kohärenten und mo-
ralisch begründeten Theorie die Abweichungen
der amerikanischen Außenpolitik von seinem theo-
retischen Ideal wie ein Seismograph registrierte:
Dabei fand er in den vergangenen fünf Dekaden
nur selten zur Ruhe. Fast niemals traf die USA aus
seiner Sicht das ideale Maß zwischen legitimer
Interesseneröffnung und notwendiger Interessenbe-
schränkung. Immer blieb aus Kennans Perspektive
darauf zu verweisen, daß die USA sich über- oder
unterschätzte. Seine Variante der "containment policy" geriet dabei zu einer historischen Alternative,
über deren Qualität heute nur noch auf theoreti-
scher Ebene spekuliert werden kann, da diese sich
nach 1949 nicht mehr durchsetzen konnte. Die
Entscheidungen zur Gründung der NATO, zur Teil-
staatsgründung in den westlichen Besatzungszonen
Deutschlands und zum Bau der Wasserstoffbombe
drängten den Direktor des politischen Planungs-
stabes des State Department zur Aufgabe seines
Amtes.
Bd. 3, 2001, 368 S., 30,90 €, gb., ISBN 3-8258-5436-1

Julia Isabel Geyer
**Rechtsextremismus von Jugendlichen in
Brandenburg**
Brandenburg befindet sich seit einigen Jahren in
den Statistiken rechtsextremer Gesetzesverletzun-
gen unter den ersten Plätzen. Zwar sind auch in
Westdeutschland rechtsextremistische Einstellungen weit verbreitet. Dennoch tritt insbesondere die
rechte Gewalt Jugendlicher in Ostdeutschland ma-
nifester in die öffentliche Wahrnehmung. Nur beide
Faktoren zusammen, Verhalten und Einstellungen,
können Aufschluss geben über die Verbreitung von
Rechtsextremismus.
Den Fragen, ob der Rechtsextremismus in Brandenburg und in Ostdeutschland insgesamt ein
spezifisches Jugendproblem ist, welche Strukturen
er annimmt, wie weit er verbreitet ist und woraus
er resultiert, wird in diesem Buch nachgegangen.
Die Analyse verschiedener Brandenburger Maß-
nahmen und Initiativen gegen rechts zeigt hingegen
trotz allem, dass es verfehlt wäre, verallgemeinernd
vom „braunen Osten" zu sprechen.
Bd. 4, 2002, 168 S., 15,90 €, br., ISBN 3-8258-6004-3

**Geschichte der internationalen
Beziehungen nach 1945**
herausgegeben von Prof. Dr. Ingeborg Koza
und Dr. Thomas Stahl

Herbert Lottner
Aufstiegswille contra Selbstbehauptung
Die Beziehungen zwischen Großbritannien
und der BRD in der Spannung von Konfron-
tation und Kooperation während der Amtszeit
Außenminister Schröders
In diesem Buch werden die Beziehungen zwi-
schen der BRD und GB in der Amtszeit von
Außenminister Gerhard Schröder untersucht. Die
Analyse geht von der politisch-psychologischen
Hypothese aus, daß GB den Status einer Macht
im Abstieg hatte, sich aber gegen den drohenden
realen oder so perzipierten Statusverlust mit aller Kraft stemmte. Die BRD wird dargestellt als
Staat im Aufsteigerstatus mit den entsprechenden
psychologischen Defekten einerseits und um so
eifriger verfolgter Überkompensation andererseits.
Der Autor legt dar wie auf dem Hintergrund einer bestimmten weltpolitischen Konstellation die
jeweiligen Ansprüche frontal aufeinander stießen
und zu einer Konfliktsituation führten.
Bd. 1, 2000, 440 S., 25,90 €, br., ISBN 3-8258-5087-0

Ingeborg Koza
**Deutsch-sowjetische Kontakte in Politik,
Wirtschaft, Wissenschaft und Kultur
1963 – 1967**
Eine Untersuchung zu den auswärtigen Beziehungen der Bundesrepublik Deutschland
Unter Berücksichtigung der weltpolitischen Inter-
dependenz erfolgt in diesem Buch eine Darstellung
der schon in den 1960er Jahren unterhalb der Re-
gierungsebene trotz aller ideologischen Gegensätze
realisierten vielfältigen Begegnungen zwischen
Menschen aus der Bundesrepublik Deutschland
und der Sowjetunion. Zu den Besuchern des je-
weils andern Landes zählten Kommunalpolitiker,
Wissenschaftler, Experten, z. B. für U-Bahnbau,
Energieversorgung, Wohnungsbau, Gesundheits-
wesen, Wasserwirtschaft, Postwesen, außerdem
Journalisten, Schriftsteller, Frauenvertreterinnen
und junge Leute. Ihre manchmal sehr subjektiven
Berichte geben Aufschluss nicht nur über das Er-
lebte, sondern auch über die Denkweise und die
politische Geprägtheit des Jeweiligen Schreibers.
Bd. 2, 2002, 168 S., 17,90 €, br., ISBN 3-8258-6212-7

LIT Verlag Münster – Hamburg – Berlin – London
Grevener Str./Fresnostr. 2 48159 Münster
Tel.: 0251 – 23 50 91 – Fax: 0251 – 23 19 72
e-Mail: vertrieb@lit-verlag.de – http://www.lit-verlag.de